HAPPY TALK

John Cox

**An exploration of what it means
to be happy and blessed**

kevin
mayhew

kevin
mayhew

First published in Great Britain in 2018 by Kevin Mayhew Ltd
Buxhall, Stowmarket, Suffolk IP14 3BW
Tel: +44 (0) 1449 737978 Fax: +44 (0) 1449 737834
E-mail: info@kevinmayhew.com

www.kevinmayhew.com

9 8 7 6 5 4 3 2 1 0

ISBN 978 1 84867 946 7
Catalogue No. 1501574

Cover design by Rob Mortonson
© Image used under licence from Shutterstock Inc.
Edited by Linda Ottewell
Typeset by Angela Selfe

Printed and bound in Great Britain

Contents

About the author

Having spent rather a long time at various universities including Cambridge, Oxford and the University College of Rhodesia and Nyasaland, John was ordained to a curacy in the diocese of Liverpool in 1968. He spent a second curacy in an inner-city ex-slum parish in Birmingham and became rector in the same parish. After a five-year period at Church House, Westminster where he was Senior Selection Secretary, helping to select ordinands, he was made Canon Treasurer at Southwark Cathedral and Diocesan Director of Ordinands and Post-ordination training.

Following four years as Vicar of Roehampton he moved to become Archdeacon of Sudbury in the Diocese of St Edmundsbury and Ipswich in 1995. When he retired in 2006 he was asked to be the part-time Diocesan Director of Education, a job he did for nearly four and a half years before retiring for a second time. It has been during these retirement years that John has been writing for Kevin Mayhew, in between being a governor at a primary academy, playing golf and enjoying river cruises.

For details of all John Cox's books, please visit our website: www.kevinmayhew.com

Introduction

I can't guarantee what will make you feel happy, but I do suggest that learning from what others have said about happiness could make a difference to your own happiness. Lots of very wise people over the centuries and from different religions across the world have put their mind to what happiness is and how we can find it for ourselves. They don't all agree but their suggestions are worth looking at to see if they ring a bell for you. So you'll find a chapter which gives a brief summary of some of those views on happiness ranging from ancient India to modern Scandinavia.

Another chapter looks at what the Bible has to say about being happy and most specifically what Jesus suggested in those sayings known as the 'Beatitudes'. As popular as they are, they often actually challenge our traditional ideas of what makes for happiness.

Being happy means we also need to understand what makes us unhappy and what we might do about it. So there's a chapter on that as well, ranging from that general feeling of misery at the state of the world, to being down because 'no one loves me'.

And to conclude, there are some practical ideas about what could make you happier. It's good to know when we are feeling miserable that there are things we can actually do about it. When we feel like blaming others, our circumstances or what's going on around us it's worth remembering what Cassius tells his friend in Shakespeare's Julius Caesar: 'The fault, dear Brutus, is not in our stars but in ourselves.' And not only faults but cures as well. Being positive, in all kinds of different ways, has the added benefit of also helping us to be happy.

1
What's it all about?

'I just want you to be happy.' I've said it to my kids. Lovers say it to each other. People say it when they fear that the advice they are giving is not going down too well. It's said in all sorts of situations. And most of the time it's simply assumed that we all know what it means to be happy. It's when you feel . . . well, happy. It's a pleasant feeling. You know . . . happy. Yes, we do know. At least we know what feeling happy means for us. We're less certain we know what will make someone else feel happy. Sometimes we are amazed at the things other people do that apparently give them so much pleasure. 'Not for me,' we say, 'but if it's what makes them happy, why not?'

Our own times of happiness, too, can actually vary greatly. Sometimes that conscious happy feeling is just a fleeting sense of joy. At other times it stretches out into what is more a sense of contentment. Seeing a stunning sunset brings a sense of delight, and reflecting on just how many things I have to be grateful for gives me a sense of being blessed. One way and another these different feelings contribute to what it means to be happy. So what is going on?

As a child I was happy playing with a cardboard box pretending it was a car. Chasing butterflies would make me happy. As an adult I don't play with cardboard boxes but I am happy driving my sports car. I don't chase butterflies or much else these days but I am happy sitting in the sun reading a book. I'm happy on my own. I'm happy sharing a meal with others. But that doesn't mean I want to do these things all the time, nor that I am always happy. There are times when it's pouring with rain, nothing seems to be going right at work, I can't get the computer to work properly and the milk in the fridge has gone sour. I'm not happy. It appears that it all depends on what is going on around me.

Worship in church can be a time of various and often intense emotion. During a funeral there are raw feelings of loss, of sadness, sometimes mixed with guilt and regrets. Weddings are, generally, times of pleasure, hope, happiness and the joy of sharing a family social occasion. A celebratory service of uplifting songs and hymns, of charismatic leadership and spiritually moving words can bring a sense of happiness that moves into bliss or ecstasy – a sense of having been blessed. A quiet service of healing or prayer can bring a feeling of peace and turn a grey day into one of pastel shades of happiness and contentment. Sometimes the simple fact of worshipping and acknowledging the presence of God is enough to give a sense of happiness. I've certainly been told on a number of occasions by someone coming out of a service, 'Thank you, Vicar. I feel better for that.'

20 March is 'International Happiness Day'! Given that most things seem to have a day devoted to them, it's not a bad thing to have one for happiness. Classic

FM marked this in 2017 by having an hour devoted to happy music – things like Strauss' *Enjoy Your Life Waltz* and Mozart's *Musical Joke*. People phoned in approvingly. Clearly such pieces made some people happy but they wouldn't have been to everyone's taste. It also happened to be Dame Vera Lynn's 100th birthday on that day. One old soldier spoke of how hearing her sing *The White Cliffs of Dover* as he sat in a POW camp had made him feel happy.

I've never been one who has madly chased after possessions. Don't get me wrong, I like to have things, but they aren't the be all and end all of whether I feel happy or not. There were times when I could have done with a bit more money. But was I miserable because I had to go without? I don't think so. However, I am conscious of the 'if only' syndrome. If only I had that, I would be happy. From what I see around me, it does look as though a lot of people do think that chasing a new possession will solve their happiness problem.

Happiness can feel a very self-centred matter. It's what I feel regardless of how others are feeling. But that is not always the case. Finding pleasure in the happiness of others is its own kind of happiness. There are times when, although it may have been difficult, we just know we have done the right thing by someone else. It feels good. We are happy to have done it, even though it may have cost us.

Do I feel happy all the time? No. I don't suppose any of us do – not even those cheerful souls who face life with a smile always playing on their lips. But nor am I what one of my friends calls 'a misery guts'. There are people who do seem happy most of the time and those who always go around with a long face. It's the way we are. Some have a happy disposition, others don't. It's the way we're made. But does that mean we can't do anything about it?

We've probably all had times when we longed to be happy and, although we weren't particularly sad, life just felt a bit drab; it had lost its glitter. It didn't feel very helpful when friends told us to cheer up. Dragging yourself up by the bootstraps seldom works but we can find that just being a bit more positive about things in general can actually help. 'I just looked at things a bit differently,' we might say. It's almost as though happiness becomes a matter of choice.

So where does all this get us? There's clearly no one thing that makes everyone happy, nor one thing alone that makes me feel happy. At any particular moment of happiness we may feel that it was a certain event or circumstance that made us happy and the temptation is to think that is the key factor for all our happiness. But that can and usually does change – not simply because the moment of happiness passes but because the next time we feel happy the reasons might feel very different.

From this brief exploration of some of the things that make us happy we can come up with some broad generalisations. We can feel happy:

- Because of things that happen around us, our circumstances

- Because of a spiritual experience, worshipping God

- Because of something we have or have just acquired, our possessions

- Because of an aesthetic experience – listening to a piece of music, for example

- Because of a social experience – sharing the joy of others

- Because of doing something that felt moral, right

- Because being happy is just the way I am, my disposition

- Because I choose to be, an act of will.

The happiness 'pie' has a varied recipe. It's not made of just one ingredient, although one may dominate at any given moment.

So happiness, it seems, is quite complex. People describe all kinds of things that make them feel happy. These might include getting out of work early to go to a football match; paddling at the seaside; listening to a favourite piece of music; hearing children laugh; a drink down the pub with mates; helping a neighbour mend the fence; Christmas; an extra slice of chocolate cake.

All of these tell us which different things can make people happy but they don't tell us what happiness is in itself. So let's see what definitions we can find. The

Oxford dictionary says happiness is 'the state of feeling happy', which doesn't get us very far. Others have described it as a state of well-being and contentment, an experience that is pleasurable or satisfying. For some people it's just a feeling that comes over you and you can't help smiling about it. Sadness would then be its opposite.

If happiness is a feeling that we all recognise when we feel it, does it really matter what it means? Will it make any difference if you don't know some abstract definition of happiness? Maybe not. But the fact is that when we are feeling sad or low, we search around for what will make us happy again. And then knowing what happiness is might be a help. If the American philosopher Don Marquis (1878-1937) was right when he said that 'happiness is the interval between periods of unhappiness' then we would all probably want those intervals to last longer and come more often. At such times it would be useful to have some idea what happiness is all about, otherwise we might be looking for it all wrong.

2

Across the world
and down the ages

This chapter is for those who like to delve into a bit of history and the way ideas develop. In this instance, the history of happiness and how it has been viewed, not only at different times but also in different places. Nothing too deep and certainly not an exhaustive survey. What you'll find here is a brief look at how the notion of happiness has changed from the time of the rise of Hinduism to the modern time, and the different ways it has been viewed in the East and in the West.

If you find being faced by a lot of ideas all at once gives you a headache, then just dip in and out of this chapter.

Although there are some marked differences in the views of happiness that we shall be looking at, there are also some recurring ideas. Just a word of caution, however. Sometimes the words used may be the same but the meaning can be a bit different. The word 'virtue', for example, has subtle differences when used in different contexts or cultures. It's a little like a colour which at a quick glance looks similar in different pictures but on a closer look you can see that the shades are not quite the same and alongside other colours can actually be quite different. It's like that here. A closer look can be worth the trouble.

Let's begin at the beginning, or at least as far back as we can.

Hinduism – freedom

Hinduism is sometimes described as the oldest of the religions. The *Rig Veda* (a collection of hymns of the Veda people) states that it began around 10,000 BCE but we've only got the *Rig Veda's* word for that. Although this Veda is the oldest of the Veda texts, it only appeared in written form about 1500 BCE.

There are problems when it comes to saying what Hinduism believes because it doesn't have a codified body of beliefs. It had no single founder and nor does it worship a single God. It comprises a range of different Indian religious traditions. However, there is a certain level of unity in that most of those traditions revere the same body of sacred texts, or Vedas. They provide an overarching framework from which it is possible to make some general statements. And that is what we have to do when it comes to answering the question of how Hinduism understands happiness.

Hinduism assumes that we humans are both bodily and spiritual beings. It is the spiritual which is the more important and the key to our true happiness. Physical and mental happiness are recognised to be good and they include things such as sensual enjoyment, freedom from worries and afflictions, a sense of fulfilment and the normal comforts of life. But none of these will bring you the ultimate happiness that lasts beyond this life. The trouble is that in chasing after such pleasures we think they are all that matters and we become attached to them, even though they don't last and don't fully satisfy us. Such an attachment is seen as a form of 'bondage'. Our everyday kind of happiness does not last; it alternates, to one degree or another, with unhappiness. And when we feel unhappy we go seeking after happiness again. It becomes a vicious cycle of happiness and misery, or what Hinduism calls dualities (*dvandvas*). We have to rise above such duality if we are to be really happy.

True happiness (*ananda*) comes as freedom from those pleasant but lesser delights of body and mind which don't last and never fully satisfy. Spiritual happiness is what we should be aiming for. That true happiness is, paradoxically, to be found as we become free from chasing after happiness.

In Hindu thinking this relates to the different aspects of what it is to be human – physical, mental and spiritual. The kind of happiness we enjoy depends on what aspect of our nature dominates.

The development of our spiritual being, and through that the discovery of our true happiness, may take some work but it is not alien to our basic nature. It is there already in our inner selves waiting, as it were, to be recognised and realised. We can't and shouldn't ignore the world around us and what it offers. It certainly isn't all misery. But we must not attach ourselves to the physical world. It is subject to change and the happiness it offers is ultimately a mirage. It is not where true happiness lies. True happiness is found in our inner selves. In the *Bhagavad Gita* (5.21), it is said: 'He who is unattached to the external world and its objects, and is attached to the inner Self, will attain supreme happiness, which is everlasting.'

This 'supreme happiness' comes from moving forward from the happiness we enjoy in this world, to the happiness we find in heaven and which is far, far better. But that also is only temporary and results in the pattern of reincarnation, which means we have to return to this world where we need to move forward again, seeking an even higher happiness. This third stage is the search for the true self, freeing ourselves from all other efforts to find happiness.

So how are we supposed to achieve this? The simple answer offered is that you need to give up desire. Free yourself from that and seek God, or your true self (which is not the same as egoism), and you will begin to discover the happiness you are seeking. Certain practices can help this:

- Love God and pray to God, so that all that you do and are is offered to God

- Serve others

- Use meditation to still the restlessness of your mind and bring it under control

- Ensure that all you say and do is 'real', 'true' – not just a facade

- Stop worrying – accept whatever comes
- Keep healthy
- Fulfil your duties and obligations
- Stop chasing happiness – let it come.

Ancient Egypt – harmony

Hunters and fishermen were living on the banks of the Nile over eight thousand years ago. They developed agriculture and animal husbandry and this led to the building of increasingly sophisticated villages and towns. Two kingdoms developed, one in Upper and the other in Lower Egypt. In 3200 BCE the northern Pharaoh, Narmer, conquered the south and united the country. Under the rule of various pharaonic dynasties Egypt retained its power for around two thousand years, after which it became divided and prey to more powerful neighbours. It fell to the Macedonians in 332 BCE.

The pyramids and the great royal tombs, along with evidence of the practice of mummification, can give the impression that ancient Egyptians were overly concerned with death, but this is misleading. They believed in the endless flow of life, not only now but continuing beyond death. This was understood in terms of harmony (*ma'at*). They celebrated the joy of life and looked for ways of ensuring that this continued into eternity. Death was a transition to be negotiated through carefully conducted rituals, allowing life to continue in a new form beyond it. But it was very important that death occurred on 'home soil' and this meant that given their power, Egyptians were not great travellers, nor creators of empires. For most people life was bounded by the village. Happiness was a matter of living peacefully, in harmony. It was not about greed or getting power.

Although there was no monolithic religious system, there were certainly plenty of gods, possibly as many as two thousand. The deities reflected what happened and was experienced in ordinary life, each having their own special area of concern, such as fertility, the hearth, beer, childbirth, cats, generosity, and love. The myriad beliefs and practices focused on the way the life of human beings and the lives of the divine interacted. Every aspect of life and nature was believed to be under the control of a deity, so if you wanted a good and happy life you had to find ways of ensuring the deities looked kindly on you. Underlying all religious rituals was the practice of magic.

As a way of producing happiness, harmony meant that people had to take into account the way that what they said and did affected the lives of others and indeed the life of the universe as a whole. This meant that the people were expected to depend on one another and maintain a balance, both in the life of individuals and in society. Not only did this make for greater happiness; it also helped to ensure that all was well when you died, allowing you to be welcomed into the Hall of Truth by Osiris, the Lord of the Dead.

Happiness as a gift from the gods came in four major ways: life, children, wealth and a proper burial.

Life meant not only a happy time in this world but an untroubled journey into the next. Having plenty of children made for happiness because they were signs of the continuation of life. This had special significance at a time when most adults died quite young. Wealth was not simply seen as the means of giving security for oneself but ensuring provision was made for one's children. To have a proper burial was vital. It had to be conducted correctly in every detail if you were to escape punishment in the next life.

Essential to all this was an attitude of gratitude. The cult of the goddess Hathor, for example, which was followed especially by the poor, emphasised and encouraged gratitude. It helped to make you happy.

Buddhism – choice

Scholars differ in their opinion about exactly when Siddhartha Gautama, the Buddha, lived and taught but it was sometime between the sixth and fourth centuries BCE. It is generally agreed that he was a prince brought up amidst the luxury of palace life in eastern India. It was when he travelled away from the palace that he first saw the life of those who lived in the villages and countryside around. What struck him was how hard their life was – so much illness, disease, suffering, and death. It led to his lifetime's search for the way we could escape from what he saw as the cycle of suffering, pain, death and rebirth.

He began by giving up all the privileges of his royal birth and became a mendicant beggar, living in the most frugal and ascetic way. This was not a particularly unusual thing to do at that time and there were several famous teachers who followed this path. They were the *sramana* – the seekers.

Gautama learnt the practice of yoga, through which he experienced high levels of meditative consciousness. But this was not enough, so next he practised extreme acts of self-mortification, to the point where people feared for his life. He was still not satisfied. He then remembered something that had happened to him as a child. Almost by chance he had experienced a particular meditative state which he now realised would lead to Enlightenment. Through the meditative practices he then followed, he discovered that they led to a happiness that did not depend on our senses.

For the Buddha unhappiness was the result of our following our cravings – the things we pursue in an attempt to find pleasure and happiness. Although they may indeed gives us times of happiness, it is only temporary, and they are replaced by unhappiness. We then imagine that it is things around us, our experiences, what we see and hear, that make for our happiness. But this is false. The truth is that real and lasting happiness is a matter of choice. We can choose to be happy. It's as simple and as difficult as that.

> Happiness is a choice, not a result. Nothing will make you happy until you choose to be happy.

No person will make you happy unless you decide to be happy. Your happiness will not come to you. It can only come from you . . . Happiness does not depend on what you have or what you are, it solely relies on what you think.
Buddha

It is a peaceful mind that brings happiness. By 'peace' is meant the freedom from cravings and desire – even from the desire for happiness itself. To attain peace, the mind needs to be purified from all negative attitudes such as greed, hate, resentment and ignorance. For Buddha ignorance didn't mean simple lack of knowledge about factual matters, but ignorance of the true nature of things; that everything is subject to change and flux. Deeply knowing this truth and living by it brings the highest state of happiness, the state of wisdom (*panna*). To reach it we need to live moral lives grounded in loving kindness for others. The Buddha was quite clear that we will never be able to show such kindness towards others unless we first show loving kindness to ourselves. True happiness will elude us. It reminds us of what Jesus was to say about loving our neighbours as we love ourselves.

Confucius – well-being for others

Confucius (551-479 BCE) lived in the Lu state (in modern Shandong province) of ancient China. His parents were what we would call 'middle class' but his father, a soldier, died when Confucius was only 3 years old and this meant he was raised by his mother in poverty. As a youngster he attended a school for commoners where the curriculum of Rituals, Charioteering, Archery, Calligraphy, Music and Mathematics (the *Six Arts*) was aimed to make him a 'perfect gentleman'. He married at the age of 19 and had three children.

Confucius worked both as a government official and as a politician, becoming state Minister for Crime at a period of considerable political upheaval. This was to influence his outlook and teaching, which drew upon religious traditions but was not itself a new religion. It was more a system of philosophy and ethics in which he emphasised the importance of being and following a good example rather than simply obeying the rules.

From our point of view, Chinese thinking in general and Confucius in particular, did not make a big thing of individual happiness. What mattered most was the part one played within the life of society, the contributions made to its cohesion and well-being. In doing so, of course, an individual could find satisfaction and happiness but that was not the goal.

At the heart of what Confucius taught is the notion of well-being – not for oneself, but for others: 'If you want happiness for a year, inherit a fortune. If you want happiness for a lifetime, help someone' (Confucius). This concern was to be shown among one's own family and friends but also more widely in society at large. It was also reflected in showing proper respect for the ancestors. Confucius encouraged people to be involved in the life of the community and in its institutions. It was also good to have fun and to be healthy if you wanted to be happy. But much more important was the requirement to do one's duty and carry out any obligations laid upon you. If people failed to do this, society could not exist in harmony and that would lead to unhappiness.

Confucius, like a number of the great teachers, had his version of the Golden Rule: 'What you do not want done to yourself, do not do to others.'

Socrates – wisdom

We now move from the Far East to the West, to ancient Greece, to have a look at the ideas of Socrates, 470-399 BCE. Nothing has survived of anything Socrates wrote. All his ideas come down to us through the writings of others, most importantly Plato. Nor can we be sure about the details of his life since historical biography, as we know it, just wasn't produced in those days. Even the exact details around the trial that led to his being sentenced to death by suicide are not certain. It is generally thought that he had been found guilty of corrupting the minds of the youth of Athens and of not believing in the gods of the state. Scholars do, however, agree about two things: Socrates had a brilliant mind and he was ugly.

As far as the West is concerned, Socrates was the first person we know of who argued that happiness doesn't just happen to you but can actually be obtained through your own effort – by becoming wise.

Plato's *Euthydemus* tells of dialogues or philosophical arguments between Socrates and a couple of brothers. Socrates argues that happiness is what we all want. It's something we aim for and is therefore an end in itself, not a means to something else. Being happy doesn't depend on things outside ourselves, like possessions or qualities or abilities, but the way we choose to use them. The obvious thing is money. Money in itself, according to Socrates, is neither good nor bad, nor will just having a pile of money guarantee your happiness. That will depend on whether you use it wisely or not. Make wise use of your money and it will make life better and happier for you. If you are foolish with your money, you are most likely to waste it and end up being unhappy. According to Plato, Socrates put it this way:

> 'Since all of us desire to be happy, and since we evidently become so on account of our use – that is our good use – of other things, and since knowledge is what provides this goodness of use and also good fortune, every man must, as seems plausible, prepare himself by every moment for this: to be as wise as possible. Right?' 'Yes,' he said.
> *281e–282a7*

So it is all down to wise choices. To help us make such choices we have to understand what it is to be truly human and which desires bring out the best in human nature, producing a sense of well-being and satisfaction. In *The Symposium* Socrates suggested that to discover full satisfaction we have to learn to go beyond loving beautiful things to the love of Beauty itself. When we have achieved that, our souls find complete satisfaction and, in a kind of rapture, we discover the truth about why we are here. This is the perfect virtue:

'. . . when a man has brought forth and reared this perfect virtue, he shall be called the friend of god, and if ever it is capable of man to enjoy immortality, it shall then be given to him (212d).

Happiness and virtue are inextricably held together. In other contexts this state of perfect virtue and happiness could be called 'bliss' or 'blessedness'.

In *The Republic*, Socrates' thoughts on happiness were developed and refined. We might summarise them in this way:

- there is a universal desire for happiness;

- we can be taught and achieve happiness through our own efforts; happiness comes, not from the things we have, but how we use them;

- setting our minds on knowledge and virtue rather than physical pleasures is what makes for happiness;

- happiness, or pleasure, is not the goal to aim for but comes through a full human life exercising virtue.

In short be wise, be good, be happy.

Aristotle – virtue and reason

Aristotle (384-322 BCE), like Plato, was a disciple of Socrates and together these three are largely responsible for creating the foundations of western philosophical thought. Aristotle had more to say about happiness than anyone else prior to the modern age. The word he used in Greek is εὐδαιμονία, *eudaimonia* and while it is often translated 'happiness', it means rather more than that. Aristotle thought that the commonly held ideas of happiness were rather crude. For him, happiness was to do with our flourishing as human beings, living virtuous lives and doing what is worthwhile. The literal meaning of *eudaimonia* indicates the idea of living according to the very best in our nature – and for Aristotle that meant following virtue or excellence. This is what life is ultimately all about. Unlike the Stoic philosophers, however, he held that external things like wealth and possessions were part of *eudaimonia*. It does, he suggests, make a difference to our sense of *eudaimonia* if we are poor or ugly or lonely. But simply being rich and beautiful and having lots of friends isn't enough for that fullest sense of happiness. These external things can all be means by which we gain happiness but happiness is not a means to something else. It is itself the goal we all aim for.

Aristotle readily acknowledged that there were various views on what constituted a good and happy life. For him it was 'virtuous activity in accordance with reason' (*Nicomachean Ethics* 1097b22–1098a20).

The important thing to remember is that for the ancient Greeks, the word 'virtue' didn't simply mean what is morally good. It had the idea of what makes for excellence in any particular activity – speed in an athlete, beauty in a fashion model, precision in a watchmaker. So virtue in the human life meant those actions that develop and reveal what is excellent in human nature. If we want to be happy it is not enough to have these qualities of excellence as potentials. We need to put them into action – and not just in any action but actions shaped by reason. Aristotle believed reason to be the crucial thing that distinguishes human beings from the animals. So it is important to develop our rational abilities. If we want to attain this virtuous, rational life which brings happiness, we have to avoid extremes. He was a great advocate of the middle way that steers a path through polarised excesses.

Friendship was very important to Aristotle when it came to happiness. It wasn't a question of how many friends you have but having the right sort – friendships based on virtue. That meant a friendship where you wanted the best for the other person, not what you could get out of it. Aristotle didn't expect people to have many such friends because they aren't easy to come by and it takes time to cultivate that kind of friendship. But at its best he reckoned friendship was even more important than either honour or even justice.

If you are asked whether you are happy, the way you answer will almost certainly depend on how you feel at that moment – 'very happy', 'not really', 'rather miserable actually'. But Aristotle would say that it is only as we look back over the whole of our life that we can really make a judgement as to whether it was happy or not, happy in the sense of fulfilling all those excellent qualities we possess in being human and having acted wisely and virtuously.

> He is happy who lives in accordance with complete virtues and is sufficiently equipped with external goods, not for some chance period but throughout a complete life.
> *Nicomachean Ethics 1101a10*

And that will take effort. It means making right choices and getting your priorities right. It means doing the right thing, not just thinking about it, or intending it. Being happy takes effort and it doesn't come easily.

Islam – worship and submission

At this point we take a bit of a leap and skip what the Bible has to say about happiness because that will have a chapter to itself. So we come now to Islam.

People think they know about Islam, but too often their ideas are shaped by what they hear through the actions of extremists. This is even true for some people's ideas about what makes a Muslim really happy. A suicide bomber, for example, is considered by the terrorists as a martyr whose 'reward' is the happy prospect of pleasure among the virgins in Paradise. It's the kind of thing that makes headlines in tabloid newspapers. So before we get carried away, it is important to look at what mainstream Islam actually has to say.

Firstly, just a word both about Muhammad (c.570-632 CE), the founder of Islam and also the context out of which the new religion arose.

Muhammad, known as The Prophet or God's Messenger, was born in the town of Mecca. As a child he was orphaned and was brought up mainly by his uncle. The wider family were prominent citizens in the city, although their fortunes were declining in Muhammad's early years. Like others in the family, Muhammad became a merchant and trader, his business taking him across large areas of the Middle East. He gained a reputation for fairness, honest dealing and being trustworthy. When he was 25, he married the first of his eleven wives.

As a young man Muhammad would often go off for a few weeks at a time into one of the local caves to pray. It was during such a time in 610 that he was visited by the angel Gabriel and given the first of the many 'revelations' or messages from God (Allah), that were later to be written down in the Qu'ran. Muhammad was considerably disturbed by that first encounter and thought people would write him off as being possessed. It was another three years before he received further revelations. These reassured him that his visions were genuine and he said he always knew the difference between his own thoughts and the messages from God.

As with so many prophets, the messages he first received were not very comfortable. They were warnings of punishment for the people of Mecca if they did not obey God's commands. At that time there were a number of gods that were worshipped and Mecca was a significant place of pilgrimage and had shrines to over 300 idols.

Muhammad's message that there was only one God and that only he should be worshipped was never going to be popular with everyone. His family and then others became his followers but he was fiercely opposed by many of the local and powerful merchants, not least because they made a lot of money out of the pilgrimage trade.

People from the other major town of the area, Medina, heard about Muhammad's preaching. Some of them met with him while on pilgrimage to Mecca and encouraged his followers to move to Medina. In 622 Muhammad learnt of a plot to assassinate him, and he and most of his followers left Mecca to emigrate (*hijra*) to Medina, where he was asked to help sort out disputes between local tribes. He continued his preaching while in Medina and the number of his followers increased substantially. At the heart of his message was the call to submit to the will of God and live obedient to his will. This gave rise to the name Islam which means submission or obedience, but which also has the meaning of peace.

Rivalry and open animosity between Mecca and Medina grew over the years with various armed skirmishes, in which Muhammad played a leading role. In 630 he headed a considerable armed force to attack Mecca. The city fell with few casualties. He was later to lead campaigns across Arabia to subdue those who opposed him and to destroy their idols.

In 632 Muhammad made his first truly Islamic pilgrimage and this is remembered in the practice of the annual pilgrimage to Mecca *(hajj)* that still exists today. Having delivered a sermon in which he exhorted his followers to remain true to what he had taught them and not to revert to their pre-Islamic ways, Muhammad returned to Medina, where he died a few months later.

As we have seen, at the core of Islam is the notion of 'submission'. Happiness, in the Islamic view, can only be understood through faith in God and a total submission to his commands, as conveyed through the messages to Muhammad and written in the Qu'ran. They ensure our happiness now but also that eternal happiness that awaits us when we die. We can know happiness by sincere worship, living virtuously, performing beautiful deeds, and by being kind and charitable.

Islam recognises that in this life there are sure to be times of hardship and sadness. That is the human condition. But seeing one's life as determined by God means that even in bad times you do not despair.

> Of the believers whoso acts righteously, whether male or female, We will surely grant such a one a good life, and We will surely reward them according to the measure of the best of their works.
> *The Qu'ran, chapter 16. 97-98*

Happiness is included in the good life mentioned here. To help ensure that happiness, the Qu'ran teaches that we should not keep comparing ourselves with others, longing to have what they have, but rather be content with what God has given us (20.131). Gratitude is important. Islam teaches that to be happy, we should be grateful to God for all that we have and whatever our circumstances (2.152). Charitable giving (*zakat*) is frequently mentioned in the Qu'ran and is one of the five central pillars of the faith. It brings happiness to those who receive and to those who give. No matter how poor or how rich one is, it is important to give to others (2.261).

To sum up: Islam teaches that there is only one God. Submission to his will in all we do, and worshipping only him brings us happiness now and, more importantly, ensures that fuller happiness of life in Paradise.

Maimonides – joy as a requirement

Known also as Ramdam, Maimonides (1138-1204), was one of the most influential Jewish scholars in his own time and since. He was born in Cordoba, Spain. When the city was conquered by Berber invaders and the protection that non-Muslims had enjoyed previously was withdrawn, the family decided to leave rather than be forced to convert. For a while they spent some time in southern Spain. Maimonides then moved to Morocco and eventually went to Egypt, where he was instrumental in raising a ransom to release Jewish captives held by the Christian Crusader King, Amalric.

Maimonides was steeped in the works of Aristotle and sought to adapt the Greek philosophy to the faith of the Hebrew Scriptures. While there was much he agreed with, when it came to the particulars of religion he parted company with Aristotle. Although widely admired, his thought was too radical for some. His thirteen principles for faith, for example, were largely ignored in his lifetime but later became obligatory for Orthodox Judaism. He was to have an influence on Thomas Aquinas.

Maimonides turned his great intellect to both astronomy and medicine but it is for his mighty fourteen volume *Mishneh Torah*, a codification of Talmudic law, that he is best remembered. It is still studied to this day.

According to the traditional Jewish law, happiness and sadness are associated with certain months of the year. It was believed that one should be happier during the month *Adar* but less happy in the month of *Av*. Maimonides omits reference to the increase of happiness during *Adar*, possibly because he believed that happiness basically depends on the nature and circumstances of each individual, whereas an attitude of sadness and mourning could be required by law. For Jews, *Av* is the saddest month of the year, during which national tragedies, such as the death of Aaron and the destruction of the two Temples are recalled.

Maimonides believed that happiness is an essential element in the fulfilling of Jewish rituals as required by God. It was not so much that performing the rituals and ceremonies made you feel happy, but that while carrying them out you should do so with joy and cheerfulness. The joy taken in fulfilling one of God's commands, *mitzvah,* and in the love of God who gives the commands, was seen as itself an act of service to God. During a Jewish holiday, rejoicing was not simply a by-product but a requirement. Maimonides ruled that to fulfil this obligation there should be wine to drink and meat to eat. That should have helped people to be happy!

St Thomas Aquinas – the vision of God

We now come to another of the most influential thinkers of the medieval period. With his grounding in Aristotelian philosophy, St Thomas Aquinas provides an interesting link between the ideas of that great Greek philosopher and the insights of the Christian faith.

St Thomas (1224-1274 CE), was born into a minor noble family in the town of Roccasecca in the Kingdom of Sicily (now the region of Lazio). His father was the Count of Aquino. Being the youngest son, it was always assumed that Thomas would follow his uncle as Abbot of Monte Cassinno. To this end, Thomas was sent to the monastery at the age of 5 to be educated by the Benedictine monks and later he went to a Benedictine house in Naples, where he also studied at the University. While in Naples two interests were to shape his future:

the philosophy of Aristotle and the new Dominican order of mendicant preachers. Thomas secretly joined the order, enraging his family who felt this was a betrayal. They had him kidnapped while on a journey to Rome. He was kept prisoner for a year, during which time his family tried to persuade him to leave the Dominicans, but he refused. After escaping, Thomas travelled to Germany, where he was ordained, and then to Paris, where he taught at the university. Although exceedingly bright, he was also very humble and this led the students to think him a dim-witted ox. His professor, however, saw just how clever Thomas was and declared: 'We call this young man a dumb ox, but his bellowing in doctrine will one day resound throughout the world.' And so it proved.

St Thomas spent his life travelling, preaching and teaching. He was a prolific writer, his most famous work the masterly *Summa Theologica*. However, in December 1273 as he was celebrating the Mass, Thomas had a vision, as a result of which he never wrote again. He had become convinced that 'all I have written is as straw to me' and he died the following year.

Key to Thomas' thinking was the conviction that reason and faith were neither opposed to one another, nor were they providing two different forms of truth. Rather, he saw faith as guiding reason and keeping it from making mistakes, while reason clarified faith.

Thomas gives considerable space in his books to the question of what human happiness actually is and whether we can find happiness in this life. In setting out his arguments, he made a distinction between the perfect happiness only possible beyond this life, when we have a direct vision of God (*beatitudo*) and the imperfect happiness we can know on earth (*felicitas*). We might see this as a distinction between happiness and enjoyment. We find enjoyment in the satisfaction of our everyday desires. Happiness comes in our attaining perfection, which can only be found in God who is himself perfect Happiness.

God, St Thomas suggested, doesn't become happy by making us. It's because he *is* happy that he makes us and makes it possible for us to share that happiness. God's happiness is simply God being God in the relationship of eternal friendship found in the Trinity (*Summa Theologica* 1-11, question 3 answer 2).

Happiness for us on earth does not come from simply pursuing what we want, but through the way we exercise reason and to the extent we live virtuous lives. To the virtues that Aristotle had identified, things like wisdom, courage, friendship, Thomas added the three theological virtues of Faith, Hope and Charity. He felt that the best way to find happiness was not by rushing around being active but through contemplation, by which we begin to participate in the perfect happiness found in being united with God. But until we obtain 'the vision of the Divine Essence' (God), our happiness will always be less than perfect (*Summa Theologica*, Articles 1-7).

So, in St Thomas' view, not only are we created by Happiness but for Happiness, that Happiness itself which is God. God wants us to share that happiness, which is himself and which we will know perfectly when we see him 'face to face'.

The Puritans – joy and mirth

The popular image of the Puritans doesn't associate them with an abundance of happiness! In fact the word is, unfairly, more commonly associated with 'kill-joys'. Harriet Beecher, the American author of *Uncle Tom's Cabin* and herself brought up within the Puritan tradition, once wrote: 'The Puritans never watered down the vinegar of life.'

The Puritans were not a distinct sect, but rather it was a name given to a number of Protestant groups of clergy and laity in England and the colonies of America in the sixteenth and seventeenth centuries. They were linked by the common belief that the Protestant Reformation had either not gone far enough or was in danger of losing its way. They wanted to purify the Church of England of what they saw as its continuing 'Catholic' beliefs and practices.

The movement began in the time of the Catholic Queen Mary, when its founders were exiled. They returned when Elizabeth ascended the throne but were unsatisfied with her Religious Settlement of 1559. It was at this time that the title 'Puritans' was first used, initially as a term of abuse, for those who wanted to 'purify' the established church. Although legal restrictions made it difficult for them to change the Church of England from within, their number grew and so did their influence, as a number of independent churches were created. They built up alliances, especially with the Scottish Presbyterian Church, and by the 1630s they were developing politically. The Puritans came to power after the Civil War of 1642-46 and the execution of King Charles I, and ruled from 1649 until 1660, when the monarchy was restored with Charles II.

Like many of the philosophers and religious thinkers we have already come across, the Puritans made a distinction between the happiness we enjoy in terms of worldly pleasures and spiritual happiness. The former they called 'mirth' and the latter 'joy'. Joy was to be found in the presence of the Lord and was exhilarating. Mirth, on the other hand, was seen to veer towards the silly, the trivial, just a matter of fun. They came down heavily on anything they thought encouraged immorality or 'lewdness'. They weren't against all forms of fun and entertainment but those that led people away from obedience to God's law. In 1642 all theatres were closed on account of the 'troublous times' and in the years that followed, increasingly stringent measures were taken against actors, who were deemed to be rogues and vagabonds. Some theatres reopened during the 1650s but since many, if not most, of the plays contained scenes the Puritans considered immoral, their opposition to them continued. They also objected to gambling, and bear baiting, and although music actually thrived in this period, they would only allow the singing of psalms in their churches.

Happiness was to be found in delighting in God, his word and his presence. Far from having long faces and 'miserable countenances' Puritans were encouraged to be cheerful, since God loves a 'sanguine complexion' (cheerful disposition). The duty of the believer was to praise God and you couldn't do that properly if you had a 'melancholy temper'. Going around being miserable, suggested the Puritan preacher Thomas Watson, was a bad advertisement for the Christian faith:

> Will others think God is such a great reward when they see Christians hang the wing and go drooping in religion? It is a sin as well not to rejoice as not to repent.

As another preacher, Jeremiah Burroughs, set out in his sermons on the Beatitudes: 'Happiness was to be found in holiness, godly mirth was to be found in praise and thanksgiving, and true joy was to be found in the Lord.'

Here is a Puritan prayer:

> O Lord,
> help me never to expect any happiness
> from the world, but only in Thee.
> Let me not think that I shall be more happy,
> by living to myself,
> for I can only be happy if employed for Thee,

and if I desire to live in this world
only to do and suffer what thou dost allot me.
*from 'The Valley of Vision' – Arthur Bennett
2003, Banner of Truth*[1]

Thomas Jefferson – happiness as a right

Thomas Jefferson, 1743-1826, was a politician, not a philosopher or theologian. As well as being one of the greatest of the American Presidents, he is best known for being the principal author of the Declaration of Independence (1776), which makes an appearance here because of the sentence at the beginning of its second paragraph:

> We hold these truths to be self-evident, that all men are created equal, that they are endowed by their Creator with certain unalienable Rights, that among these are Life, Liberty and the Pursuit of Happiness.

The Declaration set out the case for why the American Colonies were seeking to free themselves from their legal ties to England. It is worth noting that it was made when slavery was still practised in the American colonies and that Jefferson himself owned slaves. Indeed, a section of the original draft that was critical of the slave trade

---

1. From *The Valley of Vision*, a collection of Puritan prayers compiled by Arthur Bennett, copyright 1975 Banner of Truth, www.banneroftruth.org. Quoted with permission.

was deleted by Congress before giving it final approval. A later Declaration of Rights in the state of Massachusetts (1780) was similar but was seen as a legal basis for abolishing slavery.

> Article I: All men are born free and equal, and have certain natural, essential, and unalienable rights; among which may be reckoned the right of enjoying and defending their lives and liberties; that of acquiring, possessing, and protecting property; in fine, that of seeking and obtaining their safety and happiness.

Scholars are divided on what influenced Jefferson in producing his draft of the Declaration. Some see its roots in the philosophy of John Locke (1632-1704), who had argued that government existed for the sake of protecting 'property'; which he defined as a person's 'life, liberty and estate'. It is not completely clear why Jefferson changed 'property' to 'happiness'. Locke had himself viewed 'the careful and constant pursuit of true and solid happiness' as the 'highest perfection of intellectual nature' *(Essay Concerning Human Understanding)*. He also used the phrase 'the pursuit of happiness' in this same essay and although there is no way of proving it, Jefferson may have taken it from Locke. As a declared Epicurean, Jefferson would also have found the idea that happiness is the aim of life among the teachings of Epicurus (341-270 BCE), an ancient Greek philosopher.

We should not assume that in speaking of happiness, Jefferson meant exactly the same as we commonly mean by the word today. Although it can be debated, happiness in 1776 most usually means 'prosperity' or 'thriving'. Its basis was thus more associated with economic well-being than with pleasant feelings.

John Stuart Mill – the greatest happiness principle

John Stuart Mill (1806-1873), like Jefferson, had his roots in a Christian upbringing but was not a practising Christian, being agnostic on matters of faith. The world of his thought is philosophical, ethical and political.

Born in London, Mill was the son of a Scottish philosopher who decided to home educate his son with the view to making his son a genius! It was just as well he was a precocious child. At the age of 3 he was learning Greek, and Latin when he was 8, and soon reading works by people like Plato and Herodotus. As a teenager Mill studied in France, a country he came to love. While suffering depression, he considered committing suicide but was helped through this unhappy time by the poems of Wordsworth.

Brought up as a non-conformist and being unwilling to subscribe to the Thirty-Nine Articles, Mill was not able to go to Oxford or Cambridge and instead he went to work for the East India Company, while also attending lectures at London University. He remained with the Company until it was wound up in 1858. In 1865 he was elected as MP for City and Westminster and was the first Member to speak for the right of women to have a vote and often spoke in favour of social reform.

His education had partly been guided by the philosopher Jeremy Bentham, whose works he greatly admired, even though he differed from the older man on a number of points.

Bentham had held that what really drives us are the two powerful experiences of pleasure and pain, and that happiness is the greatest good. When it comes to pleasures, there is no difference between them – they are all of equal quality. The difference was only a matter of how much there was of a particular pleasure – its quantity. Chewing gum was just as good as eating an haute cuisine dinner – the only difference was how much pleasure there was. Mill and others argued that this made human pleasures no better than animal pleasures. A very long-living and happy fish could, on Bentham's view, be said to have had a better life than an average human being. While agreeing with Bentham that happiness is the ultimate good, he argued that there are qualitative differences between pleasures. Intellectual pleasures, for example, are better than sensual pleasures.

This was one of Mill's specific contributions to what is called Utilitarianism, which Bentham had first propounded. Utilitarianism evaluates actions on the basis of whether they promote happiness – not just of the individual but for the greatest number of people. Its guiding principle is 'the greatest happiness for the greatest number of people'. While most of our actions actually have various consequences – some happy, some painful, they are good actions if overall they make more people happy than sad. In measuring this, everyone counts as equal. No one person's happiness is more important than another's.

This view had developed, at least in part, from a social concern and it certainly had consequences for the way Bentham and Mill and others argued and campaigned for social reform. Some laws were felt to be wrong and it was as people considered what it was that made them wrong that this social ethic based on the happiness of the greatest number was developed. If a law leads to more people being miserable than are made happy, then it is a bad law. A law is good if it promotes the happiness of most people. It was on such grounds that Mill argued for women's suffrage and education and against slavery.

On this view it is not simply my happiness that matters but the happiness of everyone else

America – my happiness

This brief survey of what happiness has meant across the ages and in different cultures and religions has pointed up a number of differences. In a religious context there is usually a distinction drawn between the passing and inferior happiness we can know in this world and the perfect happiness to be hoped for after death. We have seen happiness as a state of mind and a matter of choice; happiness understood communally and politically; happiness as freedom and happiness as a right; happiness as virtue and happiness as a measure of good governance. The emphasis varies and the key elements differ. But there is enough similarity for us to be able to recognise what they were all on about.

So what are the emphases around these days – especially in the western world? The current obsession with happiness is actually a fair indication that people are not very happy these days. One major change in the way people view their lives and that of others has been the shift since the eighteenth century from *being* good to *feeling* good. Happiness is less understood as the consequence of good behaviour and right thinking but rather as something to be sought for itself in the balance between pleasure and pain. Indeed, we have come to think that we *should* be happy. It's our right. In order to be healthy as individuals and as a society we need to be happy. The evidence from the publishing world, from the world of motivational speakers, psychologists and therapists is that there is a preoccupation with happiness these days. It is a preoccupation which, perversely, could actually make for unhappiness in the way it sets up expectations and can make it more difficult for us to deal with and integrate painful experiences into our lives.

America may give us a clue as to what is going on. While it is probably wrong to suggest that Americans are uniquely obsessive about happiness, they certainly do go on about it a lot. And then we will look at some ideas from Scandinavia, which suggest a different perspective on the subject.

Whereas in the past, as we have seen, the acquisition of possessions was almost peripheral to the experience of happiness, it has increasingly taken up a central position. You don't have a car? Then get one, you'll be happier. You don't have blond hair? Then get it dyed, you'll be happier. You've never been on an ocean cruise? Then fork out and go on one, it'll make you happier. It's as though happiness has become attached to commodities and in a consumerist society it's the advertisers that drive that. They have created an industry out of happiness. And most significantly, it is 'my happiness' that really counts. Happiness has risen, or perhaps been forced, to the top of the expectations list.

Various reasons can be identified for this development in western culture from the nineteenth century onwards and particularly in America. These include:

- There was a decline in the commitment to Christian belief.

- Advances in material well-being – not least in those things that just made life more comfortable, many of which we take for granted these days. Having an umbrella to keep you dry, for example, or teeth that were better cared for, making you less self-conscious about smiling; each played a part.

- Increasingly it was felt that work should not simply be a grind but something you could actually enjoy.

- As jobs largely moved out of the family home there was, in the late nineteenth century, an increasing emphasis upon the way the family felt. With that came an increasing expectation that wives and mothers should make the home a cheerful place where husbands were rewarded for hard work, and children were encouraged to be successful. The downside to this was the rising divorce rate from the nineteenth century onwards which, in part, has arisen out of the failure for happiness expectations to be met.

- It was from the 1920s onwards that the vast number of books on happiness began to appear, stressing not only the importance of being happy, but also advising people how to be happy.

- Books on bringing up children emphasised happiness as against obedience. Children's happiness became a top priority.

- Companies highlighted happiness in their company literature and mottoes e.g. Walt Disney's motto was 'make people happy'.

Little surprise that we now have 'happy meals' and 'happy hours'!

Scandinavia – coffee, hugs and moderation

Intuition would probably tell us that if you want to be in a place where you are going to be happy, find the sun. Just think of all those holiday destinations in Spain, Italy or Greece. Mediterranean food, a laid-back lifestyle and hundreds of days of sun. Who wouldn't be happy? Well, apparently not the Italians, Greeks or Spaniards. At least, according to the 2017 World Happiness Report. Of the 155 countries listed, Spain comes 34rd, Italy 48th, Cyprus 65th, Turkey 69th, Greece 87th and Portugal 89th. To find happiness, go north and find the cold! Top of the happiness list is Norway; Denmark is second, Iceland third and Sweden ninth. The United Kingdom is 19th. So clearly, a country's happiness doesn't depend on cocktails on the beach. It's more likely to be a cup of coffee!

According to the Swedes (and the Finns), happiness is a four-letter word: *fika*, which means having a coffee break. While it's true that Sweden does drink a lot of coffee, and is the third highest coffee-drinking country in the world, the key thing about *fika* is not actually the drinking but the break, having a pause in the busyness of the day. In the work place this is normally twice a day, once in the morning around 10 am and then again in the afternoon. It's even better if you have a biscuit or pastry.

Fika is the opportunity, not only to stop what you are doing, easing the strain of the day, but to do a bit of socialising, having a chat with a work colleague. It's even become an institution in government offices. The idea in itself is not new, of course. Morning breaks and afternoon tea were common enough at one time in England. In schools there are still mid-morning and afternoon breaks. But all too often nowadays the cup of coffee is taken at the desk while still working – with no real chance to stop what we are doing, no opportunity to relax and have a chat, which are the very things that the Swedes find is important.

But don't overdo it. There's another key Nordic idea that makes for happiness and that's *lagom*. Basically, it means 'not too much, not too little', 'the happy medium'. *Lagom* reflects that balance and moderation which is found in Sweden and has become rooted in the Scandinavian psyche. There is confidence without cockiness, simple food but beautifully prepared, stylish design without fussiness. It makes for a balanced life without the constant demands of the smart phone, the stress of driving ambition, the striving for status. Perhaps contentment is the best word for what *lagom* produces. It's a healthy antidote to what is often seen as the excesses of life in the developed world.

One of the factors that has led to this outlook is Scandinavian socialism – that sense of the community towards which one has responsibilities but from which one receives support. Scandinavians are prepared to pay high taxes and in return they receive excellent medical attention, and care when they are old. Working hours are not excessive and there is generous parental leave. It is seen in what could be termed 'good neighbourliness'. People come together when conditions are harsh, and it has been suggested that this may, in part, account for the Scandinavian approach to social support, which contributes substantially to their happiness.

A Greek friend of mine once joked amidst all the economic problems that his country was having, that if he were prime minister, he would declare war on Sweden. It would, he assured me, be all over in a couple of days with no casualties and then Greece would become a colony of Sweden and enjoy their efficiency, their health services, and their balanced lifestyle. A happy thought, he said.

There are those, of course, who feel *lagom* has its drawbacks – not enough risk taking, or not being willing to stand out in the crowd, for instance. Perhaps it's all a bit too moderate. But then, as Oscar Wilde once put it: 'Everything in moderation, including moderation.'

There's another Scandinavian word that has been doing the rounds in the search for exactly what it is that makes for Nordic happiness. It's *hygge*, pronounced 'hooga'. If that sounds like 'hug' to you, then you're not far off the meaning. It's to do with well-being towards others and towards yourself. Give yourself a hug, it'll do you good. Do what you enjoy doing and be happy. Help others to enjoy life as well. The Danes are greatly into *hygge* but trying to pin it down is more difficult. Potentially anything you do – light candles, read a book, have friends round for a meal, go for a walk – can produce *hygge*. Whatever makes you feel comfortable, is fun and doesn't spoil things for others, is *hygge*. Its origins are to be found in ways of combatting the harshness of long, cold winters and it sounds as if *hygge* works.

So there we have it – a whizz through space and time to catch a glimpse of some of the main ideas about what makes people happy and what happiness might mean.

3

Happiness and the Bible

Off the top of my head, I would have expected happiness to feature quite prominently in the Bible. Although a fair bit of the Old Testament is given over to wars and suffering, and the misery experienced through disobedience, there are some great times as well. There is a lot of rejoicing and giving thanks – just think of the Psalms. And didn't Jesus promise us life in all its fullness – surely that means happiness? The Gospel is Good News with a promise of salvation. That's a good reason for being happy.

But when I came to look closer, things got a bit more complicated. In my concordance, which lists whenever any given word occurs in the Bible, I found 'happy' only had 22 entries – 16 translating the Hebrew *ashere* and six for the Greek *makarios*. But when these same words were translated as 'blessed' there were 70 entries. At least, that was true for a concordance based on the King James version of the Bible.

In a more modern translation like the New Revised Standard Version, things are a bit different. Apart from one occasion (Isaiah 30:18), *ashere* is always translated as 'happy' rather than 'blessed'. But with the word *makarios,* the NRSV follows the older version and uses 'blessed' – most notably, of course, in the Beatitudes. Yet, where the King James version had 'happy' for *makarios,* the NRSV puts 'blessed'. All a bit confusing.

It would seem that, while not being totally consistent about it, the more modern translations generally prefer the word 'happy' to 'blessed', reflecting a tendency, perhaps, to avoid words that might be considered overly 'religious'. Just to complicate matters further, the most recent translation, by Nicholas King, avoids both 'happy' and 'blessed' when it comes to the Beatitudes and substitutes 'congratulations' instead. Yet, for some of the Psalms he uses 'blessed' for *ashere* when the NRSV has 'happy'. In Psalm 84 he even mixes the translation, using 'blessed' twice but putting 'happy' in verse 12.

These days, 'blessed' is most often used in a religious context: the bread and the wine at Holy Communion are the 'blessed' sacraments; a building or a graveyard that has been consecrated is said to have been 'blessed'. The saints are the 'blessed'. But it is also still used occasionally in a secular way. We might say, for example, that 'this artist is blessed with a keen sense of colour' or 'the children were blessed with a loving home'. We might use it as a mild expletive to emphasise a point. 'I'm always hitting my knee on that blessed table!' In these instances, it wouldn't be so appropriate to say 'happy'. But where there is a choice, 'happy' is much more likely to be used.

Where does this geeky piece of playing about with words get us? Does it actually matter? And does it help us to learn anything about what the Bible means about happiness?

At the very least it tells me that, unsurprisingly, for the most part the Bible sees happiness in a religious context. Happiness is not so much a right or just how you happen to feel, but is a gift – from God. So, someone who has received the gift of happiness, or something that has made them happy, has in fact been blessed. The words are, to a considerable extent, interchangeable.

The Old Testament

Take, for example, Leah's expression of joy when her handmaid gives birth to a second son. 'Happy am I! For the women will call me happy' (Genesis 30:13). Leah is past child-bearing age and in the custom of the time, the child of a servant girl could be adopted as one's own. Since a woman's pride was in having children, Leah could feel happy again and the women around her would feel happy for her. Plenty of women have felt the happiness of having a child, especially when they thought it was not possible. Think, for example, of Sarah, wife of Abraham (Genesis 21:1-7) and Hannah, the mother of Samuel (1 Samuel 1:1-20) and the thousands since. In Psalm 127:4, 5, a man is said to be happy if he has a 'quiver full' of sons. However, it is not quite as simple as that. The custom referred to just now in the case of Leah, actually went out of fashion, simply because seeing the birth of a child as just a natural cause for happiness belied the deeper belief that having a child was a gift of God – a blessing. If God did not grant a woman a child, then there should not be a system of adoption to get round it. God's will, whichever way it went, was to be accepted.

Other individuals in the Old Testament are said to be happy. The Queen of Sheba was so struck by Solomon when she visited him, that she declared that the women who were his wives and the men who were his servants were happy – for they were in the presence of the great king and able to listen to his wisdom. In Proverbs, anyone who finds wisdom is said to be happy (Proverbs 3:13). Those who show kindness to the poor were also considered to be happy (Proverbs 14:21). It is less obvious how one would be happy if one was 'never without fear', as Proverbs 28:14 suggests. However, Nicholas King's translation of this verse helps to clarify what was meant: 'Happy are those who out of respect always bow [their head].' You are happy if you know your place and show respect to your betters! By and large, happiness here does not have a specifically religious context.

A man was considered happy if he had been blessed with plenty of the good things of this life – a good wife, lots of children, abundant crops, good looks, wisdom, wealth, and power. The happy man was the blessed man – a cut above ordinary folk.

However, one proverb reflects a commonly held but different view: 'Happy are those who trust in the Lord' (Proverbs 16:20). Trust was fundamental to a proper relationship with God. It brought well-being, safety and other blessings. When things are going well, when one is happy, it is not difficult to understand that one has been blessed. But, for Job, things did not go well. All kinds of calamities befell his household: his herds were stolen, fire consumed his sheep, raiders carried off his camels, and his servants were killed. To add to his woes, his children were killed when a tornado struck the house they were in, collapsing it on top of them. Even when Job was covered with sores, he did not blame God. But traditional explanations for all this misfortune didn't exactly cheer him up. Eliphaz's suggestion, 'How happy is the one whom God reproves' (Job 5:17) doesn't sound too convincing, although a similar thought is expressed in Psalm 94:12: 'Happy are those whom you discipline, O Lord.'

The Psalms

The connection between happiness and blessings is seen most obviously in Psalm 144. In verses 12-14, the psalmist lists a whole number of blessings – strong upright sons, beautiful statuesque daughters, barns filled with every produce, fields teeming with sheep and cattle heavy with young. He concludes: 'Happy are the people to whom such blessings fall; happy are the people whose God is the Lord.'

As we have seen elsewhere, not only in Proverbs, but in other religions and cultures (see Chapter 2), care for the poor is regarded as a reason for being happy and brings the added benefit of being rescued when times are dangerous. Psalm 41:1 declares, 'Happy are those who consider the poor, the Lord delivers them in the day of trouble.'

We read such passages through the spectacles of individuality, but that is to see them from the wrong perspective. A person's identity and sense of being was shaped by their place within the whole people of God and these psalms refer to Israel as a whole, rather than to individuals. It was in the people's relationship to God that their happiness (or woe) lay. So, they are happy if they come to worship and live near the temple (Psalm 65:4; 84:4).

They are happy if they are a people of trust and obedience, honouring God (Psalm 84:12; 112:1, 128:1). Israel was a people in a covenant relationship with God. He was their God, with all the benefits that would bring, so long as they were his people. Being God's people meant being a people of obedience, loyal to God alone, following his commandments, and walking in his way (Psalm 119:1, 2; 128:1).

Our view of the Law of the Lord is often shaped by what we make of those meticulous law observers, the Pharisees, as portrayed in the Gospels. All too easily, they can give us the idea that Jewish religion was dominated by hundreds of tight regulations. That is how it may have worked out in the later centuries after the return from exile, but that is not how it was intended to be.

On the one hand, we only have to read the book of Deuteronomy to see that every aspect of life was covered by rules. But in his Old Testament theology,

Walter Eichrodt[2] viewed this in a non-legalistic way. He suggests that the commandments, including the Ten Commandments, were not a legalistic code so much as a book of moral instruction. They were there to show how a people who lived in a covenant relationship, trusting and worshipping God, would behave. The primary injunction was that the people should love the Lord God with all their heart, with all their soul and with all their might (Deuteronomy 6:5). This call to love was more like a sermon than a piece of legislation. For the Hebrews, the Law was to be written in their hearts rather than in books, as the seventh century BCE prophet Jeremiah was to state later (Jeremiah 31:33). Obedience to the Law was the way to show love for God, a joy to be lived, a happiness to be experienced. This was what walking in the way of the Lord meant – for the nation and for the people who made up the nation.

Happiness, then, in the Hebrew faith was inextricably bound up with the way the people related to God and to the extent they lived in the way he willed for them. This included faithful worship ('no other Gods but me' Deuteronomy 5:7-10) and living by the moral standards set out in the Law.

Before leaving the Psalms, mention needs to be made of one Psalm that screams out to us and can rightly outrage us. I refer to Psalm 137. It is an outcry amidst the traumatic experience of exile in Babylon and begins with the sadness of those who wept as they thought of Zion:

---

2. Walter Eichrodt, *Theology of the Old Testament*, Vol. 1, SCM 1961.

> By the rivers of Babylon – there we sat down and there we wept when we remembered Zion.

But it ends with a terrifying call for vengeance:

> O daughter Babylon, you devastator!
> Happy shall they be who pay you back what you have done to us! Happy shall they be who take your little ones and dash them against the rock!

That is truly awful. It is raw passion wrung out of the Psalmist by the horrors that had been done to the people. It is a call for vengeance and, in its own terrible terms, for what was understood to be justice. For many, it is impossible to say or chant those words in a Christian act of worship. Yet it has to be acknowledged that this a cry others have echoed in their own terms and facing their own traumas down the ages. It has to be read in relation to all those calls for vengeance that we see in the Old Testament and the way that that vengeance has come to be understood within the Christian revelation.

The Beatitudes – happiness as blessing
(Matthew 5:1-10; c.f. Luke 6:20-22)

Even people who find it difficult to subscribe to such beliefs as Jesus being the Son of God, often say they follow what he taught about how we should live. As a short form, they say the Sermon on the Mount is OK but all that stuff about incarnation and resurrection leaves them cold. Without belittling this viewpoint,

I have sometimes wondered just how many of them have looked at what the Sermon on the Mount really says. Good on them if they have. It's pretty challenging.

What, for example, does it say about the things that will make you happy? Or, in more religious things, what do you need to do and be, to see yourself as blessed by God?

Before we tackle that, we need to look again at just what this opening word of the Beatitudes, *makarios,* means. There are plenty of different ways that it has been translated. The big difference is between those who put 'blessed' and those who have 'happy'. And even then, there are a number of variations on the theme: 'How blessed ...'; 'God blesses ...'; 'O the blessedness ...'; 'You're blessed ...'; 'O the bliss ...'; 'O the happiness ...'; 'Congratulations . . .'. The fact is, that the Greek word has all these possible meanings. It's a matter of which particular nuance the translator has wanted to bring out: a fairly formal religious tone, a sense of pleasant feeling, or an exclamation of joy. Each has its advantage and disadvantage.

No one word can say everything that *'makarios'* means. A translator may seek to reflect the way Jesus was understood to be using the word – which nuance was Jesus intending? Another translator may want to be sure the reader catches a meaning that resonates with them today. And Nicholas King presumably wanted that sense of joyful acclamation with his 'Congratulations'. Hence 'blessed' (and its variants) for the one, and 'happy' and its variants for the other. For our purposes, it is important that we hold the two together. Being blessed means in a deep sense also being happy. And the promise of happiness is entwined with the notion that this is a gift from God, a blessing. If we don't draw the two together, we could think Jesus was on about pious feelings that don't touch our everyday feelings, or alternatively, was suggesting a pleasant feeling that doesn't last and has no depth.

In the western world there is, generally speaking, a decline in religious adherence. There's plenty of talk about 'spirituality' in all its many forms, but commitment to a particular religious faith has become a minority activity – certainly if you measure it in terms of church attendance. A sense of God has, as a friend of mine used to put it, drained from the atmosphere. It is no longer 'the air that we breathe'. So we sometimes find it difficult to envisage what it is like to see life where God is not a question or a doubt or a puzzle, but just assumed – as naturally as breathing. The distinction that we have been suggesting between feeling happy and being blessed, and it seems to us a reasonable distinction to make, would not have occurred to people in the past. They may not have stuck with the god of their upbringing, but life without any god wasn't really conceivable. So, the religious context for happiness would have automatically been included.

We can now look in more detail what Jesus said.

Although the passage that begins with the Beatitudes is usually referred to as the Sermon on the Mount, it is most unlikely that these saying were given in one prolonged discourse. Most scholars agree that Matthew (and Luke in his turn) was drawing upon collections of sayings taken from many different occasions. Matthew wanted to present Jesus as the giver of the new Law, a second Moses figure, and so the setting of a mountain and the presentation as a single address were designed to reflect parallels with the account of Moses' giving of the Law in Deuteronomy.

The actual number of Beatitudes is normally considered to be eight. The one that comes in Matthew 5:11 has a slightly different structure and is comparable to other sayings in the Gospels that begin with 'Blessed'. It is possible that those eight were, in fact, in a slightly different order, so that there were four pairs of sayings with parallel meanings. So, for example, 'Blessed are the poor in spirit' was paired with 'Blessed are the meek'. Their parallel promises of 'theirs is the kingdom of heaven' and 'they shall inherit the earth', mean more or less the same thing – they shall share in the rule of God.

The Beatitudes turn the normal expectations of who will be blessed, who will be happy, on their head. As we have seen already, in the Old Testament to be blessed and therefore happy, was often seen in terms of wealth, good fortune, and power. Jesus subverts this approach. For him, it is the poor, the needy, the meek, and the persecuted who are the blessed, who will be happy.

Jesus is not saying that it is fun being poor or mournful. He is saying that those who don't place their expectation of happiness on wealth, on status, and on doing things their own way, are the ones who will receive the blessing of life in the kingdom of God. It is aspirational – the full blessing, the long-lasting happiness may well only come in the future but will indeed come. There's an insistence, a sense of guarantee in the way Jesus put it. It's not just a vague hope.

The poor in spirit

Luke simply has 'poor' and that may well have been the original. Matthew could see some issues arising from such a bald statement and made it more 'spiritual'. Both make worthwhile points. As we have just seen in the Jewish tradition, it was the rich, those with big fortunes, living in expensive houses who were considered blessed and therefore happy. No, says Jesus. If you follow the rule of God, not chasing after money and not relying on the riches of this world, it is you who will be blessed and will be members of God's kingdom.

It's a view we saw in various ways in Chapter 2, but here is given Jesus' particular slant. He is emphasising the contrast between what the world expects and what life in the kingdom is like. He puts it as baldly as this to shake us out of our normal way of thinking. Jesus isn't saying that just because you are poor, you are automatically a member of God's kingdom. He's talking about having the right attitude to wealth and possessions, not being attached to them, not forever chasing after them. It is possible that 'poor in spirit' refers to those friends of

Jesus who gave up their possessions, and indeed their homes, in order to follow Jesus. This reminds us that for Matthew, the Sermon on the Mount and therefore the Beatitudes, are teachings for the disciples, not the general public. In other words, the happiness and blessing promised here and those qualities and actions that receive such blessings, are characteristic of those who believe in Jesus and follow his way.

By adding 'in spirit', Matthew wanted to avoid a misunderstanding which might suggest that all that mattered was how little you had in the bank, or under the bed. He was picking up on the fact that in the Hebrew Scriptures, 'the poor' was virtually a technical term for 'the pious', 'the righteous'. So, for Matthew, Jesus is insisting that happiness is not a matter of status but of right living, following what God asks of us. The poor in spirit are not proud. They are not the ones who are confident that all that matters is their own achievement. The poor in spirit are not self-sufficient. They know that they need others. The righteous know they have need of God.

This is not a grovelling dependence, but a joyous awareness that 'all we have is thine' – as the offertory prayer has it. We are who we are and have what we have because of the goodness of God. And happy is the person who realises that. Congratulations if you have caught on to this truth. That doesn't mean we don't have our part to play or have no responsibilities, but that ultimately we can't make it without God. We aren't built to be self-sufficient and those who try to go it alone, miss out. To capture the radical nature of this saying, it has sometimes been interpreted as 'those with a broken spirit'. This is fine, so long as it is understood to mean that the spirit of self-regarding pride has been broken. It does not mean the spirit of love and adventure, courage and gratitude are to be broken. It is not a brokenness of that spirit of worth that is God's, and others', special gift to us.

What brings happiness is that the kingdom of heaven belongs to the poor, understood in these ways. They are welcomed in, they share its benefits, live its life – now in part, fully in the future.

The meek

In what was probably the original order, the meek were paired with the poor in spirit. The promise to them –'they will inherit the earth' – is simply a different way of saying 'the kingdom of heaven is theirs', which was the promise to the poor. This kind of double way of saying something is a very common feature in Hebrew sayings and writings, especially in poetry. As an example, chosen almost at random, we find this in the first verse of Psalm 24:

> The earth is the Lord's and all that is in it,
>> the world, and those who live in it;
> for he has founded it on the seas,
>> and established it on the rivers.

and in Psalm 27:1:

> The Lord is my light and my salvation;
>   whom shall I fear?
> The Lord is the stronghold of my life;
>   of whom shall I be afraid?

'Inherit the earth' means to have rule over the earth and explains what being part of 'the kingdom of heaven' means.

The meek, like the poor in spirit, are in sharp contrast to the proud and arrogant who so often appear to 'have it made', at least in their own eyes. The meek are not the Uriah Heeps of this world, always putting themselves down and making themselves a doormat to be trodden on. The meek are those with a proper understanding of their worth – a worth that is God's gift to them. Meekness does not mean delighting in a lack of proper self-confidence. It is not grovelling and pathetic. It is 'knowing ourselves as God knows us' and delighting in being a child of God. That's what brings happiness. Jesus says that the meek like this are blessed and are given, in the order to come, a place in ruling the earth.

Those who mourn

Any reference to happiness in the midst of mourning sounds grossly insensitive. There may be gratitude for all that the lost one has meant to you. There may be relief that their parting brought an end to a painful and dehumanising illness. But there is still sadness –

sometimes a devastating misery. Of all people, those who are grieving appear to be the least obvious to single out with a promise of happiness, a promise of being blessed. This feels even sharper in Luke's version where he has 'you will laugh' (Luke 6:21).

The promise doesn't suggest that mourning will automatically turn to happiness. Those who grieve are assured that there will be comfort, that consolation will be available. The implication is that for those who follow Jesus, for those who are members of the Kingdom of God, there will be comfort. In God's gracious dealing with us, even those who are hurting will be comforted and find through its blessing a way to happiness. This is the gift and the work of the Holy Spirit, the Comforter.

There is another way to understand what 'those who mourn' means. When we considered 'the poor', we saw that the term referred both to those who were poor in terms of this world's riches but also, in a more spiritual sense, to those who lived righteous lives. 'Those who mourn' can refer to those who are literally grieving the loss of a loved one. But there is also a more 'spiritual' meaning here too. What is mourned is not a loss of a life but, as it were, the loss of innocence – a grief that we are not only caught up in the whole web of sin but we are ourselves sinners. There is a sadness that we are not able to be the kind of people God wants us to be. We can all echo Saint Paul's words, that we do what we do not want to and fail to do the things we should (Romans 7:14-20). To be totally unaware that our actions and attitudes can be wrong, is be psychologically ill – to be a psychopath. To be aware that we can and do sin, is itself a kind of blessing. It is a sensitivity that keeps us spiritually alert. But it brings with it a grief that we should be like this. We sin grieving, knowing that we are also grieving God.

There is not only the sin we commit but that corporate sin that infects all people and all our world. There is the evil we see played out in the places of oppression and violence. There is the evil of injustice, abuse and prejudice. There is the sin of intolerance that cannot bear difference and there is the sin of tolerance of those wrongs that distort and damage the lives of individuals and communities. We could all add to what we see to be evil. For this, too, we mourn.

The promise that, amidst all this we shall be comforted, is more than suggesting we shall somehow be able to come to terms with it all and get over it. The promise is that there will be a new order, in which there will be an end to sin and death, to evil and hurt. And in that new order of God's kingdom there will be no reason for tears – God 'will wipe every tear from their eyes. Death will be no more; mourning and crying and pain will be no more, for the first things have passed away' (Revelation 21:4). It is also a new order of happiness.

Those who hunger and thirst

The difference between the versions in Luke and Matthew is again seen here – with Matthew amplifying what is more straightforward and down to earth in Luke. Luke has 'Blessed are you who are hungry now, for you will be filled' (Luke 6:21). Matthew says, 'Blessed are those who hunger and thirst for righteousness, for they will be filled' (Matthew 5:6).

Both share a similar underlying thought: those who recognise their need now will find life in all its fullness in the future. This was what Jesus had said he had come to bring: life in all its abundance (John 10:10). At one level, it is a promise of God's care in meeting our physical needs. But it is also a promise made to those who live their lives striving to do what is right, to live according to the will of God. We should remember that in Jewish, and therefore in Jesus' thought, there was not the sharp distinction made between physical and spiritual, as came into the Christian tradition through the influence of Greek thought. For Jesus, we are 'enspirited bodies' while for the Greeks, we are spirits entrapped in a body, from which the soul will be freed at death. However the future was envisaged, Jesus and the early Church would not have conceived it as a world of disembodied spirits. This is why, for all his reticence about the details, Paul was quite clear that beyond death we shall be given a body of God's own choosing, a spiritual body (1 Corinthians 15:38, 44). 'Bodiliness' is part of what it means to be human, now and in the future.

While we should make every effort to live morally and spiritually well, we can't actually come up to the standard God wants of us. Not on our own. This is a repeated theme in Saint Paul's writing. His distinction between the righteousness of the law and the righteousness of God underlines this (Romans 10:1-6). The one is the righteousness by self-effort, the other is a gift of God, through Christ (Philippians 3:9). It is to those who recognise their need of the gift of righteousness, that happiness is promised. Their need will be met.

The merciful

When people are asked what the big difference between the Old and New Testaments is, they are quite likely to say something about the way God was seen in the Old Testament as a God of judgement and vengeance, while in the New Testament he is a God of love and mercy. While, as in all exaggerations, there is an element of truth here, this is actually much too stark a distinction. The prophets, who were never slow in announcing God's judgement on the disobedience of the people, were also very ready to speak of God's mercy to those who sought it.

Therefore the Lord waits to be gracious to you;
therefore he will rise up to show mercy to you.
Isaiah 30:18

Let the wicked forsake their way, and the unrighteous their thoughts;
let them return to the Lord, that he may have mercy on them,
and to our God, for he will abundantly pardon.
Isaiah 55:7

> Is Ephraim my dear son? Is he the child I delight in?
> As often as I speak against him, I still remember him.
> Therefore I am deeply moved for him; I will surely
> have mercy on him, says the Lord.
> *Jeremiah 31:20*

The Psalms, the hymn book of the Temple, has frequent references to God's mercy (in modern translations this is often given as 'steadfast love').

> Be mindful of your mercy, O Lord, and of your
> steadfast love,
> for they have been from of old.
> *Psalm 25:6*

> The Lord is merciful and gracious,
> slow to anger and abounding in steadfast love.
> *Psalm 103:8*

The God of mercy also called his people to show mercy (steadfast love): see, for example, Hosea 6:6.

It is in reflecting the nature of God that we are called to be merciful. Mercy, like forgiveness, is not a denial of justice but a compassionate expression of it. Mercy does not ignore the wrong that has been done but looks with love on the wrongdoer and with the desire to bring about a transformation, a better future.

This Beatitude could appear as a kind of transaction – you show mercy and you'll have mercy shown to you. But if it is set in the context of the whole teaching of

Jesus, it can be understood in a less crudely conditional way. In the prayer that Jesus taught us there is a similar kind of condition in the call for forgiveness: 'Forgive us our sins as we forgive those who sin against us.' The gift of mercy and the gift of forgiveness are themselves what motivate us to be forgiving and merciful. If we are unwilling to offer forgiveness and show mercy to others, we will be much less likely to see the need for God's forgiveness or his mercy for ourselves. There is a dynamic in the economy of grace that is much more subtle than a simple quid pro quo. God doesn't run a slot machine for either mercy or forgiveness. They can only be understood within a relationship growing in loving forgiveness and mercy.

Part of the blessing and the joy of showing mercy to others is the discovery that even greater mercy is shown to us.

The pure in heart

Quite apart from thinking about the heart as a blood-pumping machine, we associate the heart with our feelings. It is the seat of our emotions. The loving heart, the hard heart, the forgiving heart, the joyful heart, the broken heart. Blaise Pascal, the French mathematician and philosopher once said, 'The heart has its reasons which reason knows nothing of . . . We know the truth not only by the reason, but by the heart.' We say sometimes that people are all heart, or that they go with their heart rather than with their brain when making choices. Years ago Andy Williams and Petula Clark had hits with a song called 'Happy heart' – a heart full of love.

The Hebrew understanding did not see the heart as simply the place of feelings but much more importantly as the seat of the will. It was the heart that determined what a person should do. In Exodus 35 it was the hearts of the people that were stirred to get them to make offerings to the Lord. The command to love God with all your heart (Deuteronomy 6:5; c.f. Matthew 22:37-40) wasn't a call to have especially loving feelings about God, but was a command to the people to resolutely commit themselves to God by an act of conscious will. This, too, is the force of Jesus' command that we should love our enemies (Matthew 5:44). He is not expecting us to have nice warm and cosy feelings towards those who are our enemies but to treat them well by an act of will. It doesn't mean that is easy, so much of what Jesus asks of us is challenging, but it takes it out of the realm of how we feel into the sphere of how we determine our actions.

That doesn't mean everything is automatically right. This source of our conscious will, the heart, can be duplicitous, downright evil, mixed up. It makes what we do a complex confusion of rights and wrongs, often questionable, frequently fractured. This is not the pure heart. This is not the way the pure heart acts. The person whose heart is pure is a person of integrity, single-minded in doing what is right.

So what is the happy outcome for those who have pure hearts? They will see God. The image comes from the world of the royal court. The suppliant arrives at the outer room and is required to wait. She wishes to plead her case to the king in person. Her moment comes when the usher tells her the king will see her now. She is taken into the presence of the king where she can see him face to face and he sees her. She is recognised as a person and is granted the gift of being in the king's presence.

The pure in heart are promised that bliss of being allowed into the divine presence where they can see God and be seen by him. Joy of joys, happiness upon happiness. 'For now we see in a mirror, dimly, but then we will see face to face' (1 Corinthians 13:12).

The peacemakers

In situations where unrest and protest put peace at risk, the United Nations have sometimes sent in peacekeeping forces. Parents will step in to an argument between their children in order to keep the peace. Police are deployed to keep the peace in times of riot. Peacekeeping is important. But more important, and often much more difficult, is peacemaking. Peacekeeping is a sort of holding operation. Peacemaking seeks to uncover the causes of the disturbance and bring about change. The years of war in Syria have shown just how difficult it is to make peace.

Peace in Hebrew is the word *shalom*, a word of great richness. Its meanings include harmony and completeness, as well as peace. As a greeting, *shalom* seeks these things for those we meet with. It is a desire for wholeness and well-being. This is the peace that

God offers those who respond to his greeting of peace. It is a peace that is offered to those who, in Saint Paul's terms, were his enemies (Romans 5:10). It is the loving peace that Jesus calls us to show towards those who are at odds with us. It is not a plastering over the cracks in a relationship. It's not saying differences don't matter. It isn't compromise just for a quiet life. It is an active seeking for reconciliation, for a transformation of what had gone wrong. It is not just a matter of words but of action. It can be, and often is, costly. The cross tells us that.

Those who have come to know God's peacemaking in their own lives are called to be peacemakers towards others. To be willing to take the time and effort to make peace where there was dispute, resentment, or brokenness is to find blessing and happiness. Making peace with others brings us peace, harmony, and wholeness for ourselves as well. That's something to be glad about – a sign in our lives now of what will be perfected in the future of God's kingdom. It brings us into that right relationship with God, where we are called his children. God calls us to effect what he says – we are called his children, and so we are his sons and daughters (see also Matthew 5:44 ff.), and to be a son or daughter of God means being like God.

The persecuted

The old joke says that just because I'm paranoid doesn't mean people aren't out to get me. Most of us have a sensitive spot that sends us on the defensive, feeling we are being got at when someone hits it. If that keeps on happening, we feel it's more than just hurtful; it's a kind of persecution. Prejudice can lead to a similar sense of hurt. People are persecuted just for being black, or gay, or Romany, or mentally ill. Religious extremists persecute others for allegiance to a different faith, even a different form of their own faith. These days we think this marks out Islamic extremism but the history of the Christian faith shows that followers of Christ have behaved no better on occasions.

Jesus was referring to the persecution his followers would experience. The persecution of those who lived and worked for that pattern of life which was his Way – the way of righteousness, the way of obedience to all that he was teaching. This saying resonated loudly in the life of the early Church, as Christians were persecuted, both by the Jewish and increasingly by the Roman authorities. There is nothing happy about the pain suffered through persecution. But to be a person so committed to God, so trusting that no matter what happened, he would still be with them – that would bring blessing and happiness, said Jesus. The loyalty followers showed to God would be rewarded by God's loyalty to them. This was a promise they could hold on to, even in the worst of circumstances.

The promise is nothing less than a kingdom, God's kingdom. This is not the promise of power and riches, of self-indulgence and sensual extravagance. God's kingdom is a kingdom of service and love. It is a share in that life of God's loving rule of welcome and generosity, of forgiveness and justice. In sharing God's kingdom we are promised a share in that life of God, which is the ultimate happiness and blessing.

With this promise, the Beatitudes come full circle to where they began. In the first of the sayings it was the poor in spirit who were promised the kingdom of heaven. In this last one, it is the promise to those who are persecuted.

Now and in the future

Six of the eight Beatitudes we have been looking at contain a promise for the future: will inherit, will be filled, will receive mercy etc. The force of that future tense in the original means more than simply there will be a chance of this happening. It is a promise. These things will happen. God stands as guarantor. That sounds marvellous, of course, even if that future has to wait for the time when the current order of life has been changed in the creation of a new heaven and of a new earth, or when we enter life beyond this one. It is almost as if we instinctively know that the true happiness promised by Jesus can only be known beyond this life. In that, the Christian view of things would not be so different from a number of the concepts of happiness we looked at in the last chapter. It could also be seen as further evidence for that 'pie in the sky when you die' that critics of Christianity sometimes come out with.

But as well as believing that fullness of life goes beyond what we see and experience on earth, Christianity is a 'down to earth' faith. 'Incarnation' is at the heart of the story of Jesus. The blessing and happiness God promises us may well have its fulfilment in the future and beyond this life, but it is also a joy to be known here as well. Gospel is good news because it is about the here and now and not only about some distant and different future. A 'miserable Christian' is a kind of blasphemy. And that doesn't mean, as some have assumed, that we have to go around all the time with a silly grin on our faces. It is the happiness of knowing we are held in a loving relationship. It is the happiness of knowing God believes in us, thinks we are worth all he has available, the happiness of receiving costly gifts. It is the happiness of knowing that we also have a part to play in all this. Our love, our response, our trust and faithfulness matter to God. They are part of that partnership of love which makes for blessing and happiness.

Those eight short sayings we call the Beatitudes are clues to how that partnership can work both now and in the future, and in ways that challenge all our normal assumptions of what it is that makes for happiness.

4

Unhappiness

If the Russian novelist Dostoevsky was correct when he said, 'The greatest happiness is to know the source of unhappiness', then a book looking at happiness needs also to look at unhappiness. It makes sense to think that if only we know what makes us unhappy and we are able to do something about that, we'll end up being happy. Oh that it were so easy.

For a start, there are probably as many ways to be unhappy as there are people. So we are going to have to make some generalisations. If the particular thing that makes you unhappy doesn't get a mention, then I'm sad – a) because you are unhappy, and b) because I missed out what causes you to feel miserable. And that, of course, gives us two causes – the sadness we experience because others are unhappy, and the unhappiness of failure. We'll look at those in more detail as we go along.

A worldwide issue

A feeling of unhappiness can vary from feeling a bit low to out and out depression. In one form or another, depression affects over 350 million people and is a leading cause of disability worldwide (World Health Organisation calculation). What makes so many people seriously unhappy? Is it the way they're made, the things that happen to them or have they just chosen not to be happy? While there is, no doubt, a complex mix of reasons, it is only recently that scientists have been able to identify the genetic element that is involved.

The way we're made, or not

A study of research material that looked at 280,000 people came to the conclusion that two gene variants are associated with depressive symptoms and three with happiness.[3] This doesn't mean that our genetic make-up is the only factor, but that it can play a part, at least in predisposing us to unhappiness or to well-being. There is still a lot to be discovered but it does, at least, give some credence to the intuition we have, that some people just seem more inclined to be happy or unhappy than others. It would be wrong to exaggerate this, however.

Those who are sceptical about the genetic claim will naturally emphasise all the other possible reasons, and not least the suggestion that we can actually do something about our unhappiness. Just choose to be happy. On the other hand, if genetics is, in fact, the major determining factor, then suggesting we can do things to make ourselves happier is as pointless as suggesting we can make ourselves taller just by thinking about it. This is the view of those who are critical of the whole 'happiness business' with its counselling suggestions, self-help books and focus on positive thinking.

---

3. Catherine Paddock, *Does a Happiness Gene Exist?*, Medical News Today, 7.9.2016.

It's a question of negatives

While it might be true that in the fight against unhappiness, too much has been made of how you think about things, it is widely agreed that being swamped by negatives from around us and from within, doesn't help.

Bad news

About a year ago, I changed the alarm setting on my clock radio, so that I no longer woke up to the news headlines. They were always so negative: another terrorist attack here, a domestic murder there, another case of fraud in high places, failure to get a diagnosis right at this hospital, complaints about budget reduction in schools. Why is it that bad news attracts so much attention and sells newspapers? Headlines never say things like: '91 per cent of people are delighted with the way their local supermarket treats them.' No, it's always: 'A tenth of customers complain to supermarket.' And have you noticed how statistics always get rounded up when there's a negative. We are surrounded by negatives – from the radio, from the TV, and from the papers. The situation is made worse by what is called 'fake news' on the internet and social media. The level of trust we usually have in the media is undermined. How can we be sure that what we read is real and not just some person's invention? Levels of anxiety increase and happiness declines.

So much unhappiness in the world and what can I do about it? I do my bit. I respond to appeals from the Disasters Emergency Committee but as soon as I have, then another envelope plops through the door, telling me about the plight of refugees, or the starving, the homeless or those without clean water. I can't help out everywhere, and yet doing nothing feels heartless. I get caught either way – do nothing and feel bad about it, or be concerned and still feel bad because I can't do everything. Of course, I can't, and stopping being hard on myself might be one way of feeling less miserable. Taking the world's troubles on our shoulders is one sure way of being unhappy. Trying to find a sensitive and caring balance is not always easy.

Others seem to manage it, so should I. Just look at how happy others seem. I must be a failure in this happiness business.

Making comparisons

One of the causes of unhappiness is comparing ourselves to others. The tendency is to find someone who is better than we are, make the comparison and then feel bad about ourselves. That person has a better job than I do. She is prettier than I am. He is more smartly dressed. I will never be as popular as she is. We set up ourselves for a sense of failure, so no wonder we don't feel happy. This is not the same as seeing in others something we could aspire to. Gold medal winners at the Olympics can inspire others to put in that extra bit of effort and develop a talent. Aspiration is good and too many youngsters suffer from a lack of it, ground down perhaps by those around them telling them there's no chance to improve, there's no point in getting an education. But even dreams need an element of realism about them, or we are simply setting ourselves up for disappointment and unhappiness.

Perfectionism

Jesus' injunction that we should strive to be 'perfect as our Father in heaven is perfect' (Matthew 5:48), is fine as an aspiration for living the way God wants us to. It's a goal to set before us to prevent complacency, to encourage us to be loving the way God is, but it can lead to spiritual stress and to guilt – because we know we can't be perfect. (See *It's Not Your Fault You're Stressed*, John Cox, Kevin Mayhew 2014, p 82ff.) Too many Christians have been dogged by a sense of their own inadequacy because they feel they cannot reach this goal of perfection. Too many parents have suffered guilt because they have failed to live up to the model of perfection that parenting books and gurus have set before them. There is enormous relief in a sensible regime of 'good enough'. We are much less likely to be unhappy if we accept that in an imperfect world 'if a job's worth doing, it's worth doing badly' (G. K. Chesterton).

Low self-esteem

Annie was never going to be able to please her father. He had wanted a son and had no time for his daughter. He never allowed her to be herself, but constantly put her down for failing to be the tough, athletic, rough and tumble boy he had longed for. That she was bright, artistic and sensitive were not seen as things to be admired and encouraged, but as weaknesses to be complained about. Little wonder Annie grew up thinking badly of herself, with no sense of worth, no self-confidence and no self-esteem. In her teens she frequently cut herself. She was a deeply unhappy young person during all of the years she was growing up.

Annie's experience is neither unique, nor is it normal. But many, many people, for one reason or another, suffer from a sense of low self-worth. We are told to focus on what we can do, what we are good at and not what we can't. But for many, it isn't that easy and it is only through the esteem others give to us, that we can learn to see ourselves in a new light and lose that unhappy feeling of being useless.

Lack of purpose and meaning

Dick had worked in the factory for forty years, ever since he left school at 16. He was known as a quiet, gentle man who never caused trouble, was always on time, worked well and seldom grumbled. But he didn't smile much either. If you had asked him whether he was happy doing what he did, he would have probably shrugged his shoulders. A 'not really' sort of gesture. He would have found it difficult to tell you why. 'I just wonder sometimes what was the point of it all – years of making the same kind of thing. Bits for a throwaway toy.'

We are told that hard work doesn't make us half as unhappy as work we think is pointless. Our lives need meaning, something to make it all feel worthwhile. It doesn't have to be heroic or world-shattering, but just enough to make us feel our life made a difference, was worth something to somebody. Lack that and we are unhappy.

Loneliness and being isolated

Other people can, of course, be a pain and much unhappiness comes from broken, hurtful, uncaring relationships with others. But having no one around to relate to in a close and intimate way, is to be lonely and, at worst, isolated. There's no one there for us and no one for us to be there for either. It's one of the biggest causes of unhappiness in old age. A partner dies, children move away, it's difficult to get out – and you are quickly on your own. No one is meaning to ignore you, it's just the way it is. And there is a longing to be happy again. No doubt, there are some people who feel totally at ease with their own company and have no desire to mix with others. But for most of us, being constantly on our own does not make for a happy life.

Not now

Our memories can be a tremendous source of pleasure. Whenever I go on holiday, I take my video camera with me and afterwards enjoy editing all the hours of footage into a passable film that helps me recall what we did and what we saw. I try to avoid the temptation, not always successfully, of imposing it on the family. I enjoy looking through the endless brochures from the holiday companies and planning what we might do next year. The past and the future extend the horizon of the moment and can inspire and delight the present. But to be obsessed with the past, or for ever living in the future is not a way to be happy. The past locks us into things we can no longer do anything about, and the future can become a fantasy world we strive for and never quite reach. Both can lead to a low-level dissatisfaction, an underlying sense of unhappiness in the present. Each can be an escape from the necessity of living now and dealing with what it means, now.

Unhealthy

We are constantly being encouraged to eat more healthily, take exercise, have a healthy lifestyle. Just what those things mean in detail seems to vary with the latest fashion, but that's what is expected. If we don't take any notice, we are told we will be unhappy and if enough of us take no notice, the NHS, Social Services and Community Care will be unhappy. While precise details may not be clear, there does appear to be a link between being unhealthy and being unhappy. Do we overeat because we are unhappy, or are we unhappy because we overeat? Are Americans unhappy because they eat more junk food or do they eat junk food because they are unhappy? It's not clear. But there is a link, and researchers, believe it or not, have actually shown this to be the case.[4]

Unrealistic expectations

We have seen already that striving for something we have no hope of achieving is not likely to make us happy. Although we like to think that we are in control of our expectations – it's what I expect of myself that matters – the reality is that most expectations are generated from around us. There is an increasing expectation that we should be happy, for instance. If we cannot achieve constant happiness, and we cannot, we become unhappy.

Advertisers are always on about it, with the promise that this or that product will give us happiness. So it's what we expect. But it's not realistic. The wisdom down the ages suggests that simply acquiring material possessions may produce a temporary surge of happiness, but it will not last. Chasing happiness through material possessions is a mug's game and only increases our sense of unhappiness. Once we have enough money to meet our reasonable needs, having extra makes it more likely that we'll end up feeling unhappy. It's possible that focusing on wealth and possessions as the way to find happiness merely disguises what is the real cause of unhappiness, and having the latest wall-sized TV, or an extra motor cruiser doesn't solve it.

---

4. *10 things that are scientifically proven to make you unhappy*, Anna Brech, www.stylist.co.uk

Loss

It's the bad things that happen around us and to us that we most commonly feel are the causes of our unhappiness. When it comes to comparatively small matters we are less likely to say 'I'm unhappy' than to say 'I'm not happy'. It's as though we expect happiness to be the normal state of affairs and that something going wrong stops that. But, of course, there are serious things that do cause real unhappiness. Problems with our health, not least our mental health, stress at work, loss of a loved one, being bankrupt. Any form of loss, from losing a car key to losing a pet, from losing a limb to losing our memory can seriously lower our spirits.

What do you think of if you hear that someone has 'lost control'? Did they get angry, throw their toys out of the pram and storm out of a meeting? Did they wet themselves? Did they fall asleep at the wheel and crash their car? How awful! How embarrassing! How dangerous! The thought of losing control makes us feel anxious. We feel better about ourselves if we feel we have a reasonable control on our lives. If we feel we no longer have control of our time because of the pressures others put upon us, it can make us feel unhappy. Being in a job which has no security, where the boss can get rid of you on a whim makes for unhappiness. The promise of having more say, more control in our affairs was a Brexit promise and it made people feel good. The politicians caught the sense of unhappiness about decisions being made in distant places by people we never voted for and the chance to get control again made people happy to vote to leave the EU.

As we grow older we do have less control of our lives. Physically we are less able to do things we used to do. Mentally, we worry about 'losing it'. We lose some of our contemporaries. We lose independence. Whatever the joys of growing older, of retirement – and there are any number – there are also losses. And loss can make us feel unhappy.

There are well-known stages of grieving in all situations of loss, though their intensity and duration will depend greatly on the actual circumstances. At the time it can be very hard to imagine how the dark cloud of unhappiness, or worse, will ever blow away. But, in reality, it usually does, even for those most difficult situations where, as the Americans say, there is no closure. Those parents, like the McCanns, who lose a child and never know what has happened. The wife whose husband went sailing and was never seen again. The friend whose mate just never turned up and has never been heard of since. The 'not knowing' adds to the sense of a horizon that is never reached.

Reaching the point in grief where the loss is accepted but never forgotten means that people can find happiness again. One of the reasons why some people feel unhappy for the length of time they do is because they actually feel it would be wrong to feel happy again. It would somehow be a betrayal of the one they have lost and to be a betrayer is wrong. Therefore, they feel, probably quite unconsciously, that they should remain unhappy as a sign of their loyalty or love towards what they have lost. Some psychologists, e.g. Bruce Di Marsico[5], have even gone so far as to suggest that our feelings of unhappiness result from our belief that in the face of events around us and within, we choose to be unhappy so that we don't feel bad about ourselves. In ways that reflect some of the ancient views we saw in Chapter two, the answer is to accept ourselves as we are. That doesn't mean bad things aren't bad, nor that we shouldn't aspire to be 'better' than we know we sometimes are. But it does mean being positive about ourselves, even when bad things happen.

Unhappiness can persist without us really knowing why – it's a brooding sense of sadness. It's not a clinical depression but a low mood that persists. It can be related to an event or feeling that we haven't consciously thought about for ages. It could be quite a small thing: the loss of a purse, a silly little loss of dignity, a sad story someone shared with us, or a sad film we saw at the cinema. It gets buried in our memory but underneath the surface it still makes us feel sad. And until we have in some way replaced whatever loss that event represented for us we are likely to continue to be unhappy.

Realistic unhappiness

If you have a look at some of the websites that offer advice about unhappiness, it can appear as though we have no right to be unhappy. It's our fault. We made a

5. http://www.optionmethodnetwork.com/history/unhappiness_depression.htm

choice and if only we would choose happiness, all would be well. As with so much in this area there is an element of truth in this – but it's not the whole story.

Loss is real and the unhappiness we feel with loss is real. Jesus, we must assume, made good choices about how he lived. But that didn't mean he didn't feel the loss of his friend Lazarus. 'Jesus wept', we are told (John 11:35). He would have been less than human if he hadn't. On other occasions, in the face of illness or distress, Jesus is said to have been deeply troubled. These are feelings we can share. They are real and they are natural human responses. Indeed, the more truly human we are, i.e. the more we reflect the way of being human God calls us to, the more likely we are to be sensitive to what others are going through.

So there are times when it is appropriate to be unhappy. How can we be happy about the suffering of others? Those who are, are psychologically disturbed. How can we be happy about famine and oppression? Those who are not saddened, lack compassion. How can we be happy about prejudice and injustice? Those who are not moved by such things are complacent.

There are things about ourselves too that should sadden us. We may find the Prayer Book phrase 'miserable offenders' a bit over the top but the fact is that we are sinners. Without becoming guilt-ridden, it is appropriate that we should feel saddened by the fact that we hurt others and that we fail to respond fully to God's love. The religious term is 'contrition'. When I take the time to reflect on what I do and how I am, then amidst much I am very glad about, I am also unhappy that I just don't come up to what God asks of me. What then matters is what I do about it.

It is not healthy to wallow in such unhappiness. The sadness we feel should not be a weight to drag us down into depression but a spur to set us on the path of wanting and trying to be better. For this to happen, we may well need others to help – a friend to reassure, God to forgive. So often our happiness depends on the love of others.

5

I'm H A P P Y, I know I am, I'm sure I am, I'm H A P P Y

As an 8-year-old at Sunday School I used to announce to the world how happy I felt. It was one of the many choruses we learnt at that time. We sang it with gusto and no doubt it helped us to feel happy. The 'Happy' chorus nearly always followed another one: 'Jesus loves me this I know, for the Bible tells me so.' I'm not sure how much we put our happiness down to the fact that Jesus loved us. But that's what our teacher had told us.

Just what we all made of that at the time I have no idea, but no doubt it was one of the many seeds of Christian teaching that fell on the soil and eventually sprouted into faith. To be loved, and to know we are loved, is important. There is no question that good, loving relationships have an impact on our sense of happiness, just as in the last chapter we saw that loneliness and isolation make for unhappiness. As a broad generalisation, every one of the negatives we noted there leading to unhappiness could be matched with an equivalent positive that encourages happiness. In this chapter we look at some of the ways that people have suggested could help us to feel happy. We'll be doing so with both implicit and explicit references to the Christian faith but that doesn't mean if you do not share that faith there is nothing here for you.

Change

'It's no use, it'll always be like this. What's the point of changing? Things only ever change for the worse.' If you feel like that you're in a bad way and certainly not happy. Just telling you to cheer up isn't going to help. But for most of us, most of the time, we don't feel that miserable.

If things aren't going well, if you're not feeling happy, there are two ways of looking at it – 'this is how it will always be' or 'things have got to change'. As we've already seen, there is a tendency to think that what has to change are the things around us, our circumstances, our hairstyle, where we live. But throughout the ages, the suggestion has been made that actually it is we who have to change.

Or at least we have to change how we look at things. As Shawn Achor says: 'It is not the reality that shapes us but the lens through which we view the world. If we change the lens we can change our happiness. It is not the external world that predicts our happiness but the way our brains process reality'[6]. In other words, how about looking on the bright side of things. Try looking at things more positively. Could the glass actually be half-full instead of half-empty? It is so easy to get stuck with a particular perception of things and if that is a gloomy one, then happiness will not come easily.

We could start by simply risking the possibility that change is not only possible but that change for the better

---

6. https://www.ted.com/talks/shawn_achor_the_happy_secret_to_better_work

is possible. Risk can feel dangerous but isn't risk part of what faith is all about? Faith doesn't have guarantees – it has discoveries. Faith isn't certainty – it is exploration. Happiness isn't a guaranteed outcome but it can be discovered in the process of looking on the bright side. You can't be certain that making a change will be the way to happiness but it can come as a gift.

Religion, by its very nature, tends to be 'conservative'. It likes to have things as they have been. Tradition is important. Religions resist change because they want to be true to their roots, to their Scriptures, to their long-established rites and rituals. There's an old joke: 'How many clergy does it take to change a light bulb? Change? What do you mean – 'change'?' Yet history indicates that even religions do change. There are reformations as well as counter-reformations. And one of the claims a religion like Christianity would wish to make is that it has actually been a 'change agent' in the life of society and communities through its involvement in education, social care, and justice issues. Although modern secularists would dispute it, Christians can make a strong case for the belief that overall their faith has brought good changes and increased happiness.

Be positive

Negatives make for unhappiness. Being positive can increase your chance of being happy. In a world that is often confused and confusing, full of anxiety and bad

97

news, being positive takes effort. To view the present and future in a positive light means viewing them with hope.

Hope

Hope may include being optimistic about things, but it is deeper than that. An optimist insists that everything will turn out well – and is often disappointed. A pessimist insists that, as sure as eggs are eggs, things will go wrong. It can be a protection against being disappointed because, on balance, not everything does actually go badly. The realist tries to hold the middle ground, reacting in an objective kind of way, weighing up the possibilities, good and bad.

True hope is more than just hoping for the best. It means having a realistic awareness of the way things are and bringing to that a belief in what has the power to bring about a good outcome. For some, that will mean freeing themselves from the whirligig of their desires and cravings. For others, it will mean finding that wisdom to make good choices and live good lives. For the Christian, hope may well include these things but is grounded in the action and nature of God as seen in the person, life, death and resurrection of Jesus. It draws upon the belief that God is not only ultimately in charge but that his power is one that seeks the best for his creation throughout time and space and beyond. Such hope draws the sting of the pain that life can throw at us. It sheds light on what feels dark. It draws us to that place where we can rest in the knowledge that the ultimate outcome is good not bad, is loving not hateful, is creative not destructive. It helps us to be positive, to feel happy even though there will be sad and difficult times, because in the end it is not in circumstances, nor in ourselves that hope rests but in God. As the Psalmist says:

> And now, O Lord, what do I wait for? My hope is in you.
> *Psalm 39:7*

> But I will hope continually, and will praise you yet more and more.
> My mouth will tell of your righteous acts, of your deeds of salvation all day long, though their number is past my knowledge.
> *Psalm 71:14, 15*

For Saint Paul, hope was based on the resurrection of Christ (Acts 23:6; see also Acts 26:6, 7) and grounded in the promises of the God of hope who brings peace and joy (Romans 15:13). Such promises and such hope do not, says Saint Paul, lead to disappointment because they are present in the love of God that has been poured into our hearts by the Holy Spirit (Romans 5:5).

The Christian understanding of hope makes it possible for us to live in the present with a confidence about the future. That reduces anxiety and gives cause for happiness.

Worth, purpose, meaning and control

If we lack self-confidence and have a sense that our life hasn't any real meaning or purpose, then we are not likely to feel happy. Through my work as a school governor I have long felt that a primary task for our education system is to give all children a sense of personal worth no matter what their abilities, talents, disabilities and disadvantages might be. There was a time when I was somewhat critical of those parents who said that all that mattered was that their children should be happy at school. In the face of all that education could offer, in the light of the possibilities I longed children to aspire to, under the pressure of Ofsted's demand for ever greater attainment and progress, happiness felt a bit lightweight. But over the years I have come to appreciate what happiness can mean to the individual and what it can achieve. There is wisdom in the words of the Italian physician and educator, Maria Montessori, when she said: 'One test of the correctness of educational procedure is the happiness of the child.'

Worth is one of the most important gifts that we can give to another person – a sense that they have worth, not just to others, not just to their family but worth to and for themselves. You cannot be happy if you feel worthless.

And, in part, that requires us to feel that there is purpose to what we are and what we do. One of the problems of the work some people have to do is the sense of meaninglessness. It provides an income but what difference does it really make if the world has five hundred fewer widgets? Who cares if there are twenty fewer boxes of perfectly packed biscuits? Of course, someone, somewhere may be extremely glad of a properly-made widget and well-packed biscuits are much better than crumbled ones. But at 'conveyor belt' level that may feel very distant. Amidst what can be boring and feel mindless, good management will seek to find ways that add meaning and show worth. That may in part be through the wage packet but is more likely to be successful if they offer the opportunity for involvement with others. One cake factory recently brought in a choreographer to create a simple set of dance movements for the packers to join in with, echoing the way they moved as they put cakes into boxes. It may have looked gimmicky but you could see the difference it made on the faces of the workers. That's what *fika* does for the Swedes *(see page 50)*.

I was talking recently to someone who had spent a lifetime in a job that involved caring for others. I was shocked and deeply saddened when she confided that she often wondered what good she had done in her life, 'What was the point of it all?' This was no off-hand remark. It came from someone given to careful thought and reflection. The unexpectedness of it made it all the more surprising and I just hope that further thought helped her to see that what she had done was indeed worthwhile. But that nagging feeling that we might have wasted all those years hits quite a lot of people – for some it is part of the mid-life crisis, for others a reaction to retirement. If we do not see meaning and purpose in our lives we are not likely to be happy.

One of the consequences of the decline of religious faith and commitment in the western world has been the diminishing in a sense of value that gives meaning to life. According to the World Happiness Survey, we have yet to find an alternative over-arching ethic or outlook to replace this and that has contributed to a reduction in the levels of happiness people say they enjoy.

For Christians, that sense of meaning and purpose is to be found in the belief that our lives and the destiny of the universe are in the hands of God, whose purposes are loving and meaningful. We, and all that exists, are not here by chance. The way things are is the result of the Creator's choice, not a haphazard coming together of forces and matter. Whatever the biological process of conception and birth, there is a strong sense among Christians that their very existence is itself an 'act of God' and that their lives are held within God's purpose for them. Jeremiah recorded this conviction right at the beginning of his book of prophecies:

> Now the word of the Lord came to me saying,
> 'Before I formed you in the womb I knew you,
> and before you were born I consecrated you;
> I appoint you a prophet to the nations.'
> *Jeremiah 1:4, 5*

We can discover and nurture self-confidence, purpose and meaning in ourselves but in the main it is others who help to give us such feelings, just as it is others who can undermine them. Part of loving our neighbour can be shown in the way we encourage in them a sense of worth, purpose and meaning. As we shall see later, our relationships are one of the major sources of happiness *(page 120ff)*.

Researchers have found that people who say that they are happy believe that they are in control of their lives. One of the current sources of unhappiness is the sense that it is 'they' who are in control, be they politicians, global companies, or experts. The large surge in the popular vote in America, Great Britain and France, for instance, can be partly put down to this. The call to recover national sovereignty against the domination of Brussels lay behind much of the Brexit campaign and vote. People wanted to be in charge of their lives again. They felt it would make them happier.

At a more immediately personal level, we can see this in the way we spend our time. Retired people often say that the reason they are happy not to be working is that, although they are still quite busy, they can choose what they do. They are in control, no longer bound by clocking on or off, accounting for the way every ten minutes is spent, chasing their tails to meet deadlines. Those who are always at the beck and call of their bosses, emailed day or night and even on holiday, can feel their lives are no longer theirs. As one wife complained to me: 'He's married to the job, doesn't have a moment for us or himself.' I'm not sure what that says about her view of marriage but you get the point.

However, there is a twist to this particular tale. While we can be very unhappy if we feel our lives are controlled too much by others, we do actually want others to have some control, especially over the big things. We do not want to live in a state of anarchy. We do want the country and, for that matter, the world to have shape and purpose about them. We like to think that someone has their finger on the pulse and is ensuring everything doesn't end up in chaos. Where there are terrorist threats and actions, when cyber attacks close down two thirds of the hospitals in our country, there is a cry for someone to get a grip, take control. The alternative is a high level of anxiety and unhappiness.

One of the important things that a religion does is to provide a 'big picture' that draws people together beyond family or tribal bonds. In a religion like Christianity with its belief in one God who is worshipped as Lord of all, there is the reassurance that amidst all the confusion, wonder, tragedy and joy of life, someone is ultimately in charge. Most importantly, this God is a God whose power is the power of love – not of arbitrary action, not of tyranny, not of domination. So it is, in this sense, 'safe' to acknowledge and live within the control that God exerts, both in the universal sense and in terms of our own personal lives. People put their trust in this loving God and in that love 'fear is cast out', anxiety reduced and they feel happier. In handing over their lives to the 'control' of God they discover that they do not lose the power to make their own choices but rather they find a freedom which is life-enhancing, good for well-being, and makes for happiness.

Gratitude

As the first letter to the Thessalonians comes to an end we read this:

> Rejoice always, pray without ceasing, give thanks in all circumstances; for this is the will of God in Christ Jesus for you.
> *1 Thessalonians 5:16-18*

I have heard, and probably preached, sermons based on these verses. There was no great difficulty with 'rejoicing always' and 'praying without ceasing'. But 'gratitude in all circumstances' always takes a bit of explaining. Easy enough when all is going well, when spirits are high and everything is hunky dory. But if you've just been told your cancer is terminal, been handed a redundancy notice, seen your favourite football team lose the premiership in the last minute of the last game of the season, gratitude doesn't jump readily to mind.

However, one of the things that I have consistently found while doing a bit of research for this book is the suggestion that being grateful really is a way to happiness. It's there in the words of philosophers, in the texts of religions, it's there in the books and websites of 'happiness gurus'. It has even been suggested that finding something to be grateful for every day for a month makes changes in the processes of our brains that help us to feel happier.

Gratitude requires us to be positive and, as it were, to move outside ourselves to find something to be glad about and to give thanks for. It acknowledges that we are not totally self-sufficient, nor on our own. It sees something good, no matter how bleak everything else may feel. It adds a counterbalance to all the negative news. Even if only for a moment we are caught up in the positive, we break free from the power of anxiety. We can delight in what is in others and in the world around. Telling someone else that we are grateful for what they have done is a joy to them but it adds to our happiness.

Gratitude plays a significant part in Christian worship and spirituality. When Israel went astray and drifted from their allegiance to God, the prophets and the Psalmists called them back to remember all that God had done for them and to be thankful.

> O give thanks to the Lord, for he is good;
> for his steadfast love endures for ever.
> *Psalms 106:1; 107:1; 118:1, 29; Psalm 136*

> O give thanks to the Lord, call on his name,
> make known his deeds among the peoples.
> *Psalm 105:1*

For Christians, the root of all gratitude is in what God is, what in Christ he has done and what he continues to do for us and in us. In the opening verses of so many of his letters, Paul found reason to give thanks to God for those he was writing to. Gratitude does not always come easily but we can grow in giving thanks as we draw upon the grace of God working in us (2 Corinthians 4:15).

Developing a habit of gratitude makes for happiness.

Forgiveness

Receiving forgiveness and offering forgiveness creates new possibilities. Forgiveness is not merely a wiping clean of the slate of things from the past but a positive move into the future. At best it can be transforming. Most importantly, it means we free not only others but ourselves from the spiral of guilt, resentment and anger. People may feel they are justified in their bitterness and anger towards those who have hurt them. But it doesn't make for happiness in the long term. We all know that forgiveness can be hard. We sometimes have to work hard at it. But it's worth it, not only for the way it can help to transform relationships but because it can also raise our level of happiness. It is not that we forgive in order to become happy but rather that in forgiving, and being forgiven we find we are happier.

At the core of the Christian faith is the promise of God's forgiveness and the call for us to forgive others. Whatever our view on exactly what happened on the cross, the death and resurrection of Jesus are central to the good news of the gospel and they hold the promise of God's forgiveness to us. A sense of guilt is, of course, a sign of a spiritual sensitivity that helps to guide us in recognising what is wrong and spurring us to do what is right. But guilt that overwhelms us and burdens us, and is not dealt with, diminishes our spiritual health and, indeed, can affect our physical health as well. Perhaps the most difficult of all is the sense that even if others, including God, have forgiven us, we cannot forgive ourselves. Our guilt colours our lives and corrodes our happiness. And what makes it worse is that when we feel like this we keep it to ourselves. Sometimes the manacles of guilt and misery are of our own creating when, if only we would turn to others, we might find the trust and the forgiveness to free us from them. But here, too, it can be easier said than done.

Kindness and compassion

Kindness and compassion are positives. They benefit others but they also benefit those who show kindness and compassion. Don't take my word for it. Listen to the voices across the ages, cultures and religions:

> It is the one who practises loving kindness all the time, who experiences true happiness.
> *Buddhism*

> He who is really kind can never be unhappy. If you want happiness for a year inherit a fortune. If you want happiness for a lifetime, help someone else.
> *Confucius*

> Happy are those who are kind to the poor.
> *Proverbs 14:21*

As God's chosen ones, holy and beloved, clothe yourselves with compassion, kindness, humility, meekness and patience.
Colossians 3:12

Kindness is a mark of faith, and whoever is not kind has no faith.
Islam

Three things in human life are important; the first is to be kind; the second is to be kind; the third is to be kind.
Henry James

Compassion towards self and others, acting with empathy is good. Interestingly our striving for happiness arises from selfish motivation but being unselfish is more likely to make us happy.
Thomas Plante

If you want others to be happy practise compassion. If you want to be happy practise compassion.
Dalai Lama

Body and soul

We are used to the idea that human beings are psychosomatic beings – body and mind. Outside religious circles we don't hear much about 'soul'. Efforts to identify just what the soul is, even to the point of attempting to weigh it, have usually been counterproductive. 'Spirit', however, is reasonably commonplace among both religious and non-religious people. Indeed, so common has it become that almost anything can be identified as being 'spiritual' – art, pop music, fashion, driving a car. The important point here is that in talking about happiness we need an inclusive understanding of what it is to be human. Happiness is not just about our emotional selves, although it includes that. It is not just about our social life, although that will have an effect upon our happiness. Happiness isn't just about our biological chemistry, although we should not ignore that. Happiness isn't just a matter of the state of our spirit but without reference to that, our picture will be incomplete. What's going on in our minds will also affect our happiness but it's not just a matter of our thoughts. All aspects play their part.

It may be a slightly old-fashioned phrase but 'body and soul' is a short way of saying the whole of me. In this chapter we shall be concentrating on the physical and spiritual aspects of ourselves, having had a fair look at feelings and thoughts throughout the book, and dealing with the 'social' aspects later in this chapter when we look at relationships.

Exercise and chemistry
If news items are anything to go by, it is apparent that exercise has a major part to play in our sense of well-being. We know it makes sense but when life is busy, exercise is one of the first things to go out the window.

New Year resolutions fill gyms with people determined to get fit and up their well-being. Several months on and the gyms have spare places. Knowing that exercise will help loss of weight, improve our general health and lessen our chances of heart attacks, apparently isn't enough to keep everyone at it. Less accepted is the fact that exercise reduces anxiety, stress and depression and can actually increase self-esteem and up the happiness levels. But if we want exercise to help us feel happy, we have to feel happy about doing exercise. Apparently, one of the many reasons people give for not exercising is the simple fact they don't enjoy it. Pounding a treadmill on your own can be quite dispiriting. A friend of mine had a map attached to his fitness bike and worked out a journey he would take each morning. No doubt there is an app for it these days. Exercise outdoors and with a friend increases the sense of enjoyment, although probably not on cold, snowy days. And it depends what you are wanting to get out of your exercise.

Outdoors and with a friend (especially if they are a bit fitter than you are) is great if you want to boost your fitness and general well-being. But if you are feeling stressed, anxious, or just generally unhappy, then it is probably better to do your exercise alone, indoors, in a more relaxed, even contemplative way. Exercise alone won't suddenly increase happiness but it does contribute. It can stimulate the creation and distribution of certain chemicals in our bodies, and especially in our brains, that help us to feel happier.

When we take exercise we should have an aim in mind – a two-mile run, a shorter time than we took last time,10 press-ups, five minutes without stopping. The goals don't have to be world shattering. Indeed, it's better to achieve a series of small goals regularly than try something big but only occasionally. Setting a goal and achieving it releases a chemical called dopamine, which has been variously described as the 'happiness drug' or the 'reward molecule'. When you achieve a goal, there's a good feeling. You feel happy. That's what dopamine is doing. And give yourself a little celebration. Apparently that's important.

Did you feel good when you exercised? Was there a sense of achievement? Feeling you have value, have done something significant, whether or not related to taking exercise, boosts the levels of another chemical called serotonin. It makes us feel good about ourselves. Because of the way the brain works, serotonin flows whether we have an actual sense of achievement and worth at this particular moment, or whether we remember such an occasion from the past. Most of us have at some time or another been praised, especially thanked for what we have done. If you are feeling down, think back on that time, remember what it felt like. Your serotonin levels will go up and you'll feel happier. Neurochemistry tells us what common sense already knew. Thinking positively about ourselves lets the happiness in.

I'm not a great one for hugging people. A polite handshake or a quick peck on the cheek is usually enough for me. Too much enthusiastic hugging at the Peace in church always feels a bit OTT. But if I want to feel happier, I've got it wrong. Hugging is a bonding, intimate kind of action and what that does is release oxytocin, the so-called 'cuddle hormone'. Dr Paul Zak, a world expert on oxytocin, suggests we have eight hugs a day. Mothers release this hormone when they breastfeed, and it is also active when having sex. It helps build up trust, intimacy and healthy relationships. Even the simple matter of receiving a gift will do it. Good levels of oxytocin help us to feel happier.

The last of the four so-called happiness chemicals is endomorphines. They are released when we feel depressed or are in pain and are there to help deal with it. The 'high' that runners get after a vigorous run comes from this. For those not given to such energetic practices there is good news – having a good laugh, or even anticipating a good laugh will up the levels of your endomorphines. It's not simply that being cheerful already makes you feel happier but it releases the chemical that helps to sustain that feeling.

As scientific knowledge increases concerning the way our bodies behave, it becomes obvious that happiness has a hidden but real physical component. Among the many things that influence how we feel, the chemicals inside us have a part to play. We aren't aware of them but we feel the results of their presence or absence. Neither is automatic. We can make choices that will help their release or that will inhibit their flow. We can choose to exercise or not. We can choose to set ourselves goals and celebrate our achievements or not. We can choose to cut ourselves off from other people or we can seek to build good relations with others. We can be po-faced if we want but we can also choose to have fun and have a laugh. The sages of old knew nothing about dopamine or endomorphines but they did tell us happiness is a matter of choice.

Christianity has had a mixed attitude towards our bodies. On the one hand they are the gift of God. They are, in Saint Paul's phrase, temples of God (1 Corinthians 3:16). But our bodies are also the residing place of lusts and desires that are in conflict with the spirit within us. All kinds of spiritual and physical practices have sought to keep the body under control – from flagellation to fasting. The Incarnation, the Word becoming flesh (John 1:14) is a sign of the significance of the physical nature of being human. Whatever the exact nature of the resurrection will be, the Apostles Creed affirms that there is resurrection of the body. So our physicality matters. What we choose to do with our bodies is not neutral. Those choices have clear moral and spiritual consequences. That they can also affect our happiness is not irrelevant to what it means to be a Christian.

Meditation and mindfulness
Knowing that I had written a book about stress and depression, my son sent me the weblink to Shawn

Achor's TED talk on Happiness and Success.[7] Among the five ways Achor suggests for being happy, I was surprised to find not only gratitude and kindness but also meditation. It was the prompt for this book. Here was a psychiatrist speaking at a meeting of secular business people and some of what he said resonated with ideas that I was more commonly used to finding in Christian writings. It made me want to explore more and that led to this book. Such are the quirks of authorship.

We have already looked at gratitude and kindness so now it is the turn of meditation.

There must be thousands of books written about meditation – what it is, how to do it, which method to follow, its place in particular religions and world views. I am no expert. But as a Christian I start from two simple places: a verse from a Psalm and a prayer.

The verse is from Psalm 46 and is very well known:

> Be still and know that I am God.
> *Psalm 46:10*

And the prayer is the one known as the Jesus Prayer. It comes from the Orthodox Church and appears in various forms. The one I have used is:

> Lord Jesus Christ, Son of God, have mercy on me, a sinner.

---

7. www.ted.com/talks/shawn_achor_the_happy_secret_to_better work?language+en #t-507070

They are for me reminders, points of focus and attention, a way of drawing my mind to the things of God and letting go.

One of the things that leads to stress and general feelings of unhappiness is the frantic rush of busyness. And noise. Not just the noise of traffic and radios, of chatter and music played too loudly but the noise in our heads. It's the noise of all those thoughts chasing around, of expectations and targets, of demands and data. It's the noise we need to get away from, for at least part of each day.

'Be quiet,' says the Psalmist. Take time out, relax, put all that cries out for attention to one side for a few moments. It can wait. Take the weight off your feet, with all their rushing about. Find a place and a time when you will not be disturbed. Sit quietly with the weight of your body evenly distributed, your feet at rest on the ground, your back straight but not rigid, your muscles relaxed, your eyes shut and your breathing gentle. Still the mind and attend to just one thing – the way you breathe, a picture, a cross, a flower, a prayer. Your choice. Like it or not, there will be thoughts rushing for attention. They come unbidden. Just put them quietly to one side, nothing aggressive and return to what you were focusing on. If you've never tried this before, don't attempt too much. Just a few minutes, but try each time to lengthen the period until you have found a length you feel comfortable with, you feel refreshed by, and you feel quietened by. These are moments of retreat

– of withdrawing your attention from all that goes on around and refocusing it within.

The Psalmist goes on to say 'and know that I am God'. In the meditation of a person of faith, the inward attention is drawn to the God who is within us, as well as Lord of all. It is a time of 'knowing', not with the intellect, trying to sort out doubts and questions, but the knowing of being with someone whose presence we relax into and discover. It is the knowing of trust and relationship.

Meditation, we are told, helps all sorts of conditions, not least anxiety and depression. It's good for our well-being and that includes our happiness. Just how you meditate is your choice; there are any number of ways and any number of aids.

One of the ancient aids to meditation is the mantra – a short phrase frequently repeated either out loud or to ourselves. This is where the Jesus Prayer (Lord Jesus Christ, Son of God, have mercy on me, a sinner) comes in. It can be used as a Christian mantra, quietly focusing the mind in the rhythm of its repetition and the reassurance of its words. It speaks of the promises of God and his Son and it acknowledges the reality of who I am – not to build guilt, for it speaks of mercy even before the admission of sin. It states simply and straightforwardly what I am. No kidding about myself, no airs and graces. A reality check. But it also tells me that in the mercy of God I am a forgiven sinner. And that is an important reality too. The prayer reflects the nature of the relationship of love between who I am and who God is.

I remember a special time when I used this prayer. It wasn't the way meditation is normally practised. I was not alone. I was not sitting quietly. It was an hour shortly before dawn and I was slowly but steadily climbing the steps from Elijah's plateau to the top of Mount Sinai. The rhythm of the prayer and the rhythm of each step became for me a time of meditation as we approached the summit where we would celebrate Holy Communion. It was a time of joy and happiness.

If meditation is a movement of our attention from external to internal, then mindfulness might be described as a movement of our attention from the past and future to the present. Although it's rooted in meditative practices from the past, especially Buddhism, mindfulness has these days become all the rage. An item on the news recently highlighted a school in Surrey where all the pupils practise mindfulness each day. They said it helped them to be less anxious about the upcoming SATS tests.

It is all too easy to live looking back to the past or anxiously wondering what the future will bring. The advice to Lot's wife not to look back was wise, and not heeding it did her no good at all. The past can fill us with regrets – things we did, things we failed to do. We can be haunted by past guilts and bear the wounds of past conflicts. What is coming up on the horizon can also be a source of anxiety, not least because we don't know for sure just what it will be. We worry about what will happen if . . . , we are anxious about an appointment, anxious about what we will be expected to do, anxious about meeting strangers, visiting strange places, eating strange food. Spending too much time looking back or anticipating the future means we lose the energy and the attention needed for this moment. We lose too its enjoyment, its achievement, its happiness. Be in the present, focus on the now without judging – that is the message.

Omar Khayyam, the tenth-century Persian poet said:

> Be happy for this moment. This moment is your life.

And a millennium earlier Seneca had his own view:

> True happiness is . . . to enjoy the present, without anxious dependence upon the future.

Mindfulness has many exponents and advocates. In some circles it is *the way* to help your well-being. But it is not without its critics. The past is not simply filled with regrets and bad moments. It also has wonderful memories, it has times of achievement that support our self-esteem, it holds stories to share that build relationships. It gives us access to our personal, cultural and religious roots. To avoid all thought of the future would mean no planning, no delightful anticipation, no aspiration towards a vision of what might be. So while there is much that is helpful about mindfulness, it has to be tempered with common sense.

Togetherness

There's a Charlie Brown cartoon that I have often quoted. Lucy is pouring scorn on Charlie's intention to be a doctor. 'You could never be a doctor,' she says. 'You know why? Because you don't love mankind, that's why.' 'I love mankind,' Charlie insists, 'it's people I can't stand.' I guess there are times when all of us have had some sympathy with that. People can really get you down sometimes. As a clergy friend of mine says, 'When I'm on holiday I just want to get right away, not just from the parish but from people in general.' And he's a caring pastor.

Some relationships can be wearing or even damaging, but one of the things that is repeatedly said in any discussion of how we can be happy is this: 'You're less likely to be happy on your own and certainly not if you feel isolated.' That doesn't mean you have to rush around making loads and loads of friends. That's not the answer. It's the quality of relationships that matter – close, intimate, trusting and caring relationships. George Sand, the French novelist reckoned there was only one kind of happiness – to love and be loved.

In the Judeo-Christian tradition there is considerable emphasis on the importance of showing 'brotherly (and sisterly) love'. Both traditions are fundamentally communal faiths, where the individual has importance but the priority is upon the community of the faithful – the people of Israel and the new Israel. That community is bound together by many strands – the worship of a common God, a set of commands and regulations, the bond of shared stories, and a sense of obligation to one another.

> How very good and pleasant it is
> when kindred live together in unity!
> *Psalm 133:1*

In his first letter, John has some strong words to say to both those who show brotherly love and those who don't:

> Whoever says, 'I am in the light', while hating a brother or sister, is still in the darkness. Whoever loves a brother or sister lives in the light, and in such a person there is no cause for stumbling.
> *1 John 2:9, 10*

Saint Paul, writing to the Christians in Corinth, was concerned about reports of quarrels among the congregation and appealed for the brothers and sisters to live in unity:

> Now I appeal to you, brothers and sisters, by the name of our Lord Jesus Christ, that all of you should be in agreement and that there should be no divisions among you, but that you should be united in the same mind and the same purpose.
> *1 Corinthians 1:10*

The foundation of such a community did not rest in people merely agreeing with one another but in the shared belief, and their fellowship through baptism 'in Christ'. What they held in common with one another was much more important than their differences. And as far as Paul was concerned, that included differences of gender, race, class and status (Galatians 3:28).

We may pride ourselves in being independent but the reality is that we all depend on others. The vast majority of them we never know – they grow and pack and transport our food, they work the generators so we have electricity, they build our houses, they clean our streets. They make life possible because none of us can do all that is needed for modern living on our own. But what sustains our being at a deeper level, what makes for deeper well-being, are those fewer known and close relationships. They are the people we feel enough at ease with to admit our vulnerabilities and our needs. They are the people from whom we gain our sense of worth. They build our self-confidence. They make us feel happy.

Worthwhile, sustained relationships don't just happen, not even for those who fell in love after just a glance. Relationships take work. It is true for the relationships we have with family and friends and it is also true for our relationship with God. Regular prayer, worship, fellowship and study of the Scriptures – these are the 'tools' for building and sustaining our relationship with God. They help us to be open to God and to be open to what God offers us, through the power of his Spirit. They bring us closer to God. Trusting, loving, close relationships – they are part of the recipe for a happier life.

Be real – about yourself and your expectations

If you want to be truly happy in that sustained way that leads to contentment, it's no use living in a fantasy world with inflated expectations and an unrealistic view of yourself. That doesn't mean don't have dreams. That doesn't mean don't aim high. It means that we don't lose sight of what is real. I might aspire to be the world's strongest man but that's not real – certainly not at my age, and in fact it never was. But it might be for someone else. Being real doesn't mean putting ourselves down from what we can actually achieve. It means a realistic assessment, plus a little more, because most of us are actually able to achieve more than we think we can and sometimes a lot more.

When all that is said, the fact is that if we have unrealistic expectations we are simply setting ourselves up for disappointment and unhappiness. We lose out on the happiness that achievement brings and experience the pain of unrealised dreams. There's no guarantee, of course, that even realistic expectations will always be met. Part of life is having to learn how to deal with shattered dreams. My granddaughter dreamt of being on the West End stage as Matilda. She went through a whole series of auditions, getting more excited as she passed each stage. But there came the point when she was no longer called out. Her dream was shattered – and it hurt. These are things we have to learn from and move on. Part of the 'happiness industry' is the illusion it can give that we can be happy all the time, or we should be happy all the time. If we aren't, someone is to blame: ourselves, others, God.

...and about happiness

We may think that there's nothing unrealistic about wanting to be happy, but the fact is we are not going to be happy all the time. Chasing after perpetual happiness is a mug's game and will only end in tears. In fact, chasing happiness at all is pretty pointless. Happiness comes as a gift. It is a by-product of other things, other choices. We choose to be positive, to be kind, to be forgiving, to exercise and with a bit of luck, happiness will come along riding in their wake. We worship, we say our prayers, we give thanks to God, not with the primary aim to be happy but find that through our worship and our prayers and our gratitude, there are times when happiness smiles upon us.